choreographing space

e+i studio

Artifice

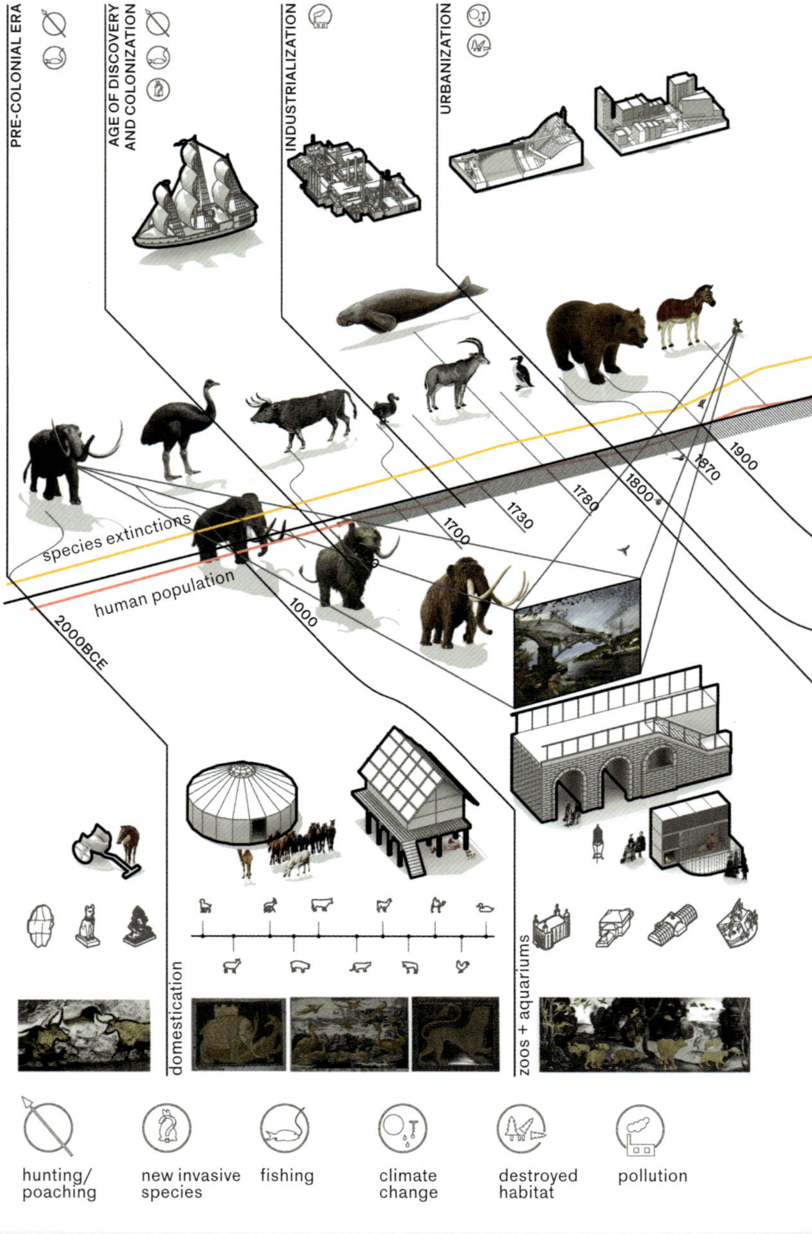

PRE-COLONIAL ERA
AGE OF DISCOVERY AND COLONIZATION
INDUSTRIALIZATION
URBANIZATION
species extinctions
human population
2000BCE
1000
1700
1730
1780
1800
1870
1900
domestication
zoos + aquariums
hunting/ poaching
new invasive species
fishing
climate change
destroyed habitat
pollution

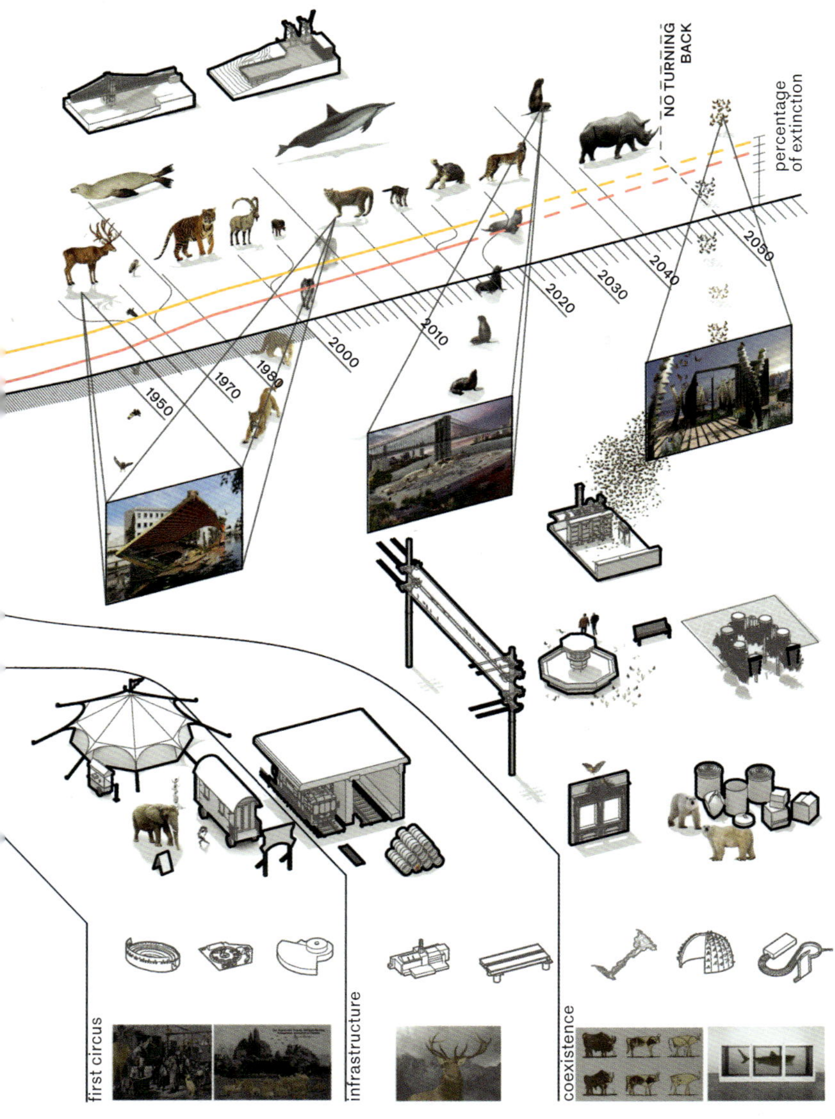

animal extinctions and architectural typologies timeline

contents

Foreword | Jesse Reiser + Nanako Umemoto + Julian Harake

As espoused through the work of Eva and Ian, the reception of architecture—even the reception of its representations—is rather a full-fledged bodily experience: an engagement of all the senses. Although this claim is nothing new, such requisite sensitivity to the workings of art and architecture are increasingly all too rare. Against the hypersonic tempo of contemporary life, architecture takes time both to produce and feel in its fullest sense. It is why the most sensitive architects tend to be of an older generation, with the impatience and hurry of youth often left unrewarded. It is also why, we suspect, so many young architects are drawn to the instant gratifications of image culture. As doing so eschews the hard work of architecture toward the final result of its representation, by consequence much of today's work can be categorized less as architecture and more as propaganda. As a counterpoint to image culture, philosophical texts have been used by Eva and Ian to frame conceptual architectural ideas.

By necessity, a book on architecture is usually one of images, and thus exists the tendency to take architecture for an image: to reduce it to the renderings, photographs, drawings, and diagrams through which it is represented while not considering as much as one could the material presentational substrate—the actual architecture—from which such images emerge. The converse, whereby architecture is born through images, is a similar story. Sophisticated drawings and fantastical renderings can often be translated into subpar buildings, only to then be augmented through photography for print and online distribution. These can be compelling in a book or on a screen; however, the results of such procedures unfailingly fall flat when seen in person, comprising but the naïve results of surface-level thinking.

What to make then of the speculative work, temporary pavilions, and performance—the "choreographed spaces"—of e+i studio as represented through the documents of this book, all highly dependent upon the movement of visitors —sometimes dancers, and the occasional mammoth or cougar—in and around them through time? We have two ideas. One is more pedestrian and pragmatic: say that, although their performances may be over, work left unbuilt, and pavilions packed away, we can at least glean some sense of what they were and might be through their documentation—the typical, compensatory means of presenting architecture through print. We prefer another answer, however, and think it truer to the work of Eva and Ian. Like fiction, architecture need not be real nor built but simply believable; like fairy tales and fables, and unlike the world we currently inhabit, architectural representations need not be imbedded in reality but rather in the possibility of reality. The difference is subtle yet crucial: whereas one is bound to represent

represent and propagate the world as is, the other acts as a springboard for the imagination and as hope for other ways of living.

Even if known, such advantages of fiction are seldom utilized by architects, and it is here that Eva and Ian distinguish themselves. In their proposal for an eyewear showroom, we are told that the project would "most likely [become] engulfed" with plants, rabbits, and not just butterflies but "Karner blue and monarch butterflies". Elsewhere, as part of an entryway into New York's Chinatown (adjacent to their home and studio), Eva and Ian write of how the eastern cougar and short-eared owl might "flourish" in their architecture, along with no small number of American lotus peppers.

As with all good fiction, it is the attention to detail with regards to the actual architecture, its affording possibilities, and those species that might inhabit it —human or otherwise—which allows one to enter it. Fantasy strongly anchored in common histories and what is already known: a kind of magical realism for our material world.

To paraphrase one such distinguished American writer, "writing is but the careful release of information over time". As that author, Toni Morrison, might attest, such care and choreography are lifetime commitments, "not gifts to society but rather its necessity". The same goes for the unbuilt and actualized fictions of Eva and Ian, who have devoted themselves, carefully, project by project, to the design and articulation of new forms of architecture. Against the fashionable grain of their contemporaries, the virtues of such patience lie herein.

This book is a reflection around a selection of projects from our collaborative practice as e+i studio that is both retrospective and speculative. Retrospectively, it explores the people, places, and practices that have influenced our projects, a revisiting that allows us to see new linkages between works across time, as well as re-evaluate their significance. As a future-oriented speculation, the book also proposes posthuman scenarios for some projects, to support the idea that any reflection on architecture must necessarily involve a reckoning with the ecologies it affects.

The book's organization emerges from an effort to "speciate" our projects, much like when living creatures are categorized into seemingly related groups under their genus. We identified conceptual strands of each project and organized them under headings, or species, which were further clustered into the four parts that structure the book. The effort here is to use these groupings to synthesize ideas and intents, knowing that it could always be done differently. Nothing is static, or definite; we see our projects as being in a continuous process of becoming, as they question relationships to evolving ecologies of thought and thoughts on ecology.

Each of the four parts—Flow, Engage, Gather, Perform—opens with a philosophical text that acts as a prelude to the topics, reflections, and questions generated by the projects. Each part is concluded with a speculative scenario where one of the projects is imagined in a future where nonhuman life, which is now endangered, is thriving in the future. These are not intended as nostalgic or apocalyptic scenarios, but rather as affirmative alternatives to the current bleak collective imaginary given the climate crisis of our own making and the continued exclusion of nonhuman life in the built environment.

This book aims to be accessible to many different readers, as it can be engaged with in entirely different ways: as a philosophical inquiry by focusing on the texts that frame each of the four parts of the book; or one could completely bypass the philosophy and enter into the projects themselves, the places, people, and circumstances that affected them; or even take the more speculative route with the posthuman life that some projects are given, reflecting on our condition as one species among many and the repercussions this has for the way we practice architecture moving forward.

A special place is given to the thought that students will find something of value in this publication. As partners of e+i—Eva Perez de Vega and Ian Gordon —we have been continuously engaged in teaching alongside our practice. It is with students in mind that we reflect on the state of our profession, the need to engage with climate justice and offer an affirmative look at how seemingly unrelated disciplines such as dance, philosophy, and skateboarding can contribute to the many unexpected avenues architecture can take you down.

The book is also a recognition of the influence and the engagement we have both had with movement-related practices that have always traveled in parallel to our architectural work: dance & skate. While the work is highly collaborative, it is also very much a result of lived experiences, which are often intimately tied to disciplines tangential to architecture.

We have to acknowledge the role of the urban landscapes that sustain us as people and as a practice. Firstly, Rome, the city where we met as school kids, starting our partnership well before either of us trained as architects. Next, New York City, where we expected to stay for two years, but twenty years later this is still the place where we—like most who feel foreign in their own cities—feel at home, and Chinatown, a place with a culture that we embraced, and that has allowed us to move outside of our innate Eurocentric thinking.

A special acknowledgment goes to the many collaborators who have been an integral part of our work: Ziyu Chen, Susana Chinchilla, Aviva Novick, Erika Hrivikova, Sidhant Seth, Hakan Westergren, Andreas Fernandez, Jonathon Koewler, Flavia Bertorello, Jacinda Ross, and especially to Yotam Ben-Hur, whose enthusiasm and personal involvement in the earlier stages of the book produced a first manuscript. And to the dancers with whom I shared many training hours at the Martha Graham studio, and who later became collaborators: Eva Perrotta, Sophie Bortolussi, Kristina Skovby, Maya Sørensen, and the extraordinary dance teacher Kim Jones. We are grateful to the friendships that have started through professional collaborations: to Yana and Harry Schnitzler for our continued friendship that began with the project that gives name to this book; to Jesse Reiser, Nanako Umemoto, Debbie Reiser, and Daniel and Nina Libeskind for showing us that great architecture can be done with kindness and generosity, and a special thanks to Nanako and Nina for being so supportive during trying times.

To our daily reminders that we need to rethink the way we tread on this planet, Siena and Yan, thank you for adapting to our live-work lives and making it a seamless joy. This book is dedicated to the memory of Sumac Caceres and to the special bond we will always have in our mutual passion for dance and architecture. Lastly, we are always grateful to the ongoing dialogue with our students, in the parallel practice of teaching, which continues to inform our outlook on architecture and its critical role in a changing world that demands radically different ways of intervening in it.

flow

choreographing space

strada dinamica

jeongok prehistory museum

eyewear showroom

10

The body of architecture and its images

The technical reproduction of images has eviscerated something fundamentally corporeal to the appreciation of artwork and its architecture. Experiencing an artwork in the flesh requires a full body commitment; even when the artwork itself is two-dimensional, the experience itself is three-dimensional. It always requires physical presence and bodily engagement; whether it is walking toward it, around it or looking up to get a better view. One would have to engage with our body's kinesthetic capacity to appreciate the work or get a full picture of the meanings and techniques behind the image. When an artwork is integrated into a built space, such as frescos and plastered paintings, conditions for viewing may not be optimal. Sometimes the spatial configuration may impede a full view, or the lighting conditions might not be equal throughout, which may cause strain to the viewer. As such, it also demands the engagement of senses other than the visual: the smell and tactility provided by the architecture that houses it, as well as our sense of balance and orientation, all contributing to the experience of the artwork image.[1] An increased awareness of its architecture, how integral the artwork is to the space that supports it, contributes to the appreciation and communicative capacity of the artwork itself.

An artwork that cannot be reproduced is, by its very irreproducibility, demanding of the viewer a commitment to engage with it by using all our senses, and not only the visual register. Given its bodily dimensions, the artwork is essentially understood as three-dimensional, because that is the only way to experience it; with the body, with motion. Even frescos, which are two-dimensional, are not ever really experienced as such, because they are always intimately tied to the architectural space that houses them and by the bodily movement needed to appreciate them.[2] An artwork becomes dissociated with its physical architectural space once it is reproduced and exhibited elsewhere, or seen in a book or on a screen.

This shift in viewing modes—in the spectator and in the space—and the resulting loss of dimensionality from technical and digital reproducibility can be explored by zooming into three moments in history with a glance into the changing conception of images, and our relationship to them and the space that contains them.

I Unified body

The way artwork is displayed and images are appreciated goes hand in hand with the conception of the architecture that houses them. Leaving aside for the moment the important distinction between building and architecture, our built environment has always played a pivotal role in the way we appreciate artwork.

The influential writer and cardinal of the counter reformation Gabriele Paleotti, who set the church's views on the proper role and content of art in his *Discourse on Sacred and Profane Images*, is key to understanding the critical role that images played prior to the Renaissance. For Paleotti, images could communicate more rapidly than text and reach a much wider audience, they are more immediate and transformative—powerful tools that have the ability to *convert*.

During this time and prior to the possibility of reproducing images photographically or by other technical means, images are artworks built into the spaces of churches and public buildings, integral to the architecture that houses them. As such, one *experiences* these images just as one experiences a three-dimensional space; there is a clear parallel between the experience of a space and the experience of the artwork integrated within it. One is meant to "educate" the other; to enhance their communicative capability with such force as to be able to, according to Paleotti, have the capacity to change people's belief systems. In this sense the images of Christianity were three-dimensional because they were tied to the three-dimensional space that contained them. As soon as images can be reproduced in two-dimensional form, they lose the third dimension and with that they eviscerate something very essential to how humans experience the world—with our bodies.

In his treatise on architecture, Vitruvius's discussions on proportions for architecture in Book Three are dominated by the analogy with the perfectly proportioned male body, known mostly through the translation into an image drawn by Leonardo da Vinci almost a millennium later, the *Vitruvian Man*.[3] Interestingly, the new life given to his text in the Renaissance via illustrations often embodied an agenda quite distinct from that of the Roman architect.

Da Vinci's drawing and the subsequent versions, which have been exhaustingly reproduced, invariably show a standing naked man, actively illustrating the proportional relationship between the body and geometrical figures of a circle and a square. It is an undeniably three-dimensional body, but it is worth paying closer attention to Vitruvius's original words:

> *For if a man be placed flat on his back, with his hands and feet extended, and a pair of compasses centered at his navel, the fingers and toes of his two hands and feet will touch the circumference of a circle described therefrom. And just as the human body yields a circular outline, so too a square figure may be found from it. For if we measure the distance from the soles of the feet to the top of the head, and then apply that measure to the outstretched arms, the breadth will be found to be the same as the height, as in the case of plane surfaces which are perfectly square.*[4]

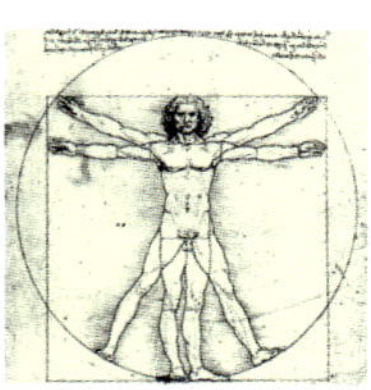

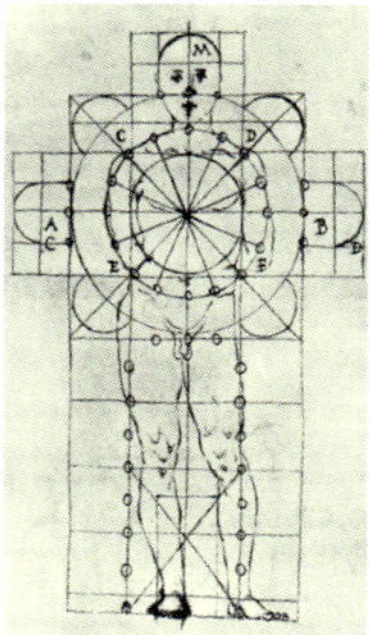

While the *Vitruvian Man* of the Renaissance is invariably illustrated as a standing figure, Vitruvius's description clearly has the man lying down—"placed flat on his back"—in a more abstract disposition. He is a two-dimensional geometric figure used to illustrate proportion and symmetry. The fact that Vitruvius's description had the man lying down indicates a direct correlation between the idealized proportions of the human body and the regulating geometries of the floorplan. His purpose seems to be that of providing a planimetric organizing tool—a diagram—something to be mapped on a floor plan for the correct layout of its proportions. In a sense, the man described by Vitruvius is more abstract and two-dimensional than the three-dimensional standing image produced in the Renaissance. We do not know what the drawing would have been like had it been drawn by Vitruvius himself, but we do know it would have had a more direct relationship with a floor plan than with an elevation, close to the illustration made by Francesco di Giorgio Martini, where the body is quite literally inscribed inside the floor plan of a church.

Curiously, what may be obscuring Vitruvius's words is in fact illuminating the humanistic concepts of images from the Renaissance. Illustrating the *Vitruvian Man* as standing instead of lying down is also a consequence of the invention of perspective, a technique of drawing that mimics the human cone of vision elevating the human point of view to a privileged position in artwork. With perspective, the subject's particular point of view becomes the central and dominant organization of space, and thus the change of emphasis from floor plan to perspective seems a natural one, as does a tight correspondence between the human body and architecture.

II Disembodied body

For Vitruvius and Renaissance masters inspired by his writings, man was the unifying body of architecture. This ingrained notion, however, did not remain uncontested. If, as Vitruvius tried to teach us, the unified body of architecture is that which understands the tight-knit connection between the human body and the physical spaces that encompass that body, then a disembodied body emerges when the threads that keep them together begin to unravel, and one starts to dissociate from the other.

This seems to be what happened at the beginning of the twentieth century with the possibility of reproducing images by technical means. The rapid reproduction of images allowed for the almost complete dissociation between the artwork and the space where it was being shown. There was a loss of what Walter Benjamin calls the "aura"; the connection that all images have when coupled with the space that houses them: "Even the most perfect reproduction of a work of art is lacking in one element: its presence in time and space, its unique existence at the place where it happens to be."[5] Furthermore, the intent seems to be to push this dissociation to the extreme, whereby it involves not only the dual relationship between the space and the artwork, but also the three-way relationship that comprises the space, the artwork, and the subject appreciating the artwork. So, how does one disembody a subject?

With the mechanical reproduction of artworks, sight much more dominates the other senses, which are intentionally excluded; spaces become flatter; and sound is then a negative aspect of these spaces, as are texture and other sensorial variations. A particular behavior also seems to be required, conditioning our experience of the work. Often referred to as an "aesthetic device",[6] the gallery for viewing images and the auditorium for viewing moving images have the capacity to deeply condition our attitude toward the artwork.

There is still a persistent conception that the optimal way to view works of art is in a white box, and, conversely, in a black box for movies. These are understood as neutral backgrounds designed to incite a specific behavior of reverence and ritual in the viewer. When entering such spaces, one tends to know how to behave; lowering one's voice and quietly focusing on that which is meant to be viewed. There is an assumption that there is a singular "right way" to experience a movie defined by a particular relationship between the image or moving image, the spectator, and the physical environment that houses them. We associate these environments with the artwork without realizing that it took many decades and many variations before we landed on these seemingly stable typologies and for them to establish themselves as the singular way of consuming still and moving images.

Interestingly, these two typologies seem to have paralleled themselves in time, and what is referred to as the golden age of the "white box" coincided with the most glorious season of the "black box", from the 1920s until the 1970s.[7] The crisis that the work of art has gone through with mechanical reproduction is similar to that of the cinema, now that its golden age is behind us. Much like artworks, movies can now be experienced without the apparatus of the movie theater auditorium and can instead be streamed on tablets, computers, and phones, which has put the act of going to the cinema in crisis.[8] The art gallery or the auditorium can profoundly influence the viewer's reaction to the content being housed or shown, by imposing precise styles of viewing and of listening.[9] What is the optimal physical condition for spaces that house images and how are they designed to induce in the spectator a specific kind of behavior and elicit a particular kind of experience?

II.I The emergence of the white-box space for images

The architecturally integrated artwork of the sixteenth century gave way to the "picture gallery" of the eighteenth century, where the work of art was used to adorn and enhance interior spaces. Thus, while full integration

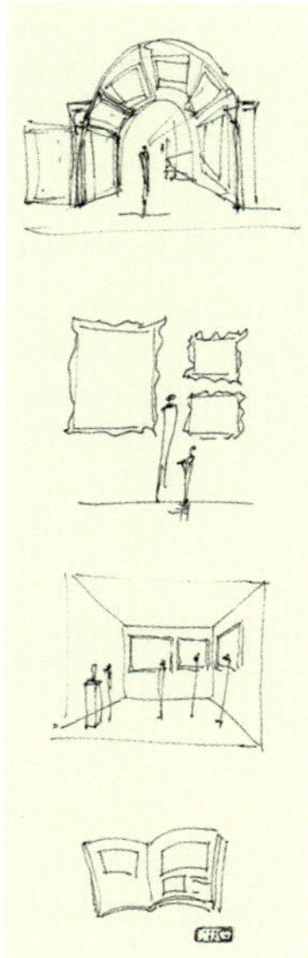

was no longer dominant, there was a reciprocal relationship between the space and the image contained in it insofar as one is used to enhance the other: the picture adorned the space, the space enabled the picture to be contemplated within a particular environment, or aura, around it.[10] However, this relationship is no longer held by a tight fit as the two are no longer codependent. There is a slight dissociation between the space and the artwork: the artwork gets framed allowing for its easy transportation and relocation, making the space that houses it become associated with temporality rather than permanence. Images and space for contemplation of images are no longer coupled together as was the case with frescoes of the Renaissance or mosaics of the Middle Ages in religious and public places. As a consequence, the space loses dimensionality, as exemplified by the typology of the white cube.

The loss of dimensionality in the image and in the experience of the image or artwork went hand in hand with a *flattening* of the space that housed them. The rapid reproduction of images at the beginning of the twentieth century with photography allowed for almost complete disassociation between the artwork and the space where it is being shown. In losing the authenticity, there is also a loss of what Walter Benjamin calls the "aura"; the connection that all images have when coupled to the space that houses them:

> *Even the most perfect reproduction of a work of art is lacking in one element: its presence in time and space, its unique existence at the place where it happens to be.*

With this separation between image and space, there is a distancing between the spectator and the image, giving way to the typology that is most taken for granted, the white cube. Here, the walls, ceilings, and floors are deprived of any color beyond a neutral white or gray, resulting in complete dissociation between the artwork and the space. As we arrive to the white cube as an aesthetic device of modernity, it becomes more specifically about vision, and not the complete sensorial experiencing which the architecturally integrated artwork of the sixteenth century demanded. This typology seems to be designed to have a specific ritualistic effect on the viewer; a sense of reverence toward the images on the wall and a complete negation of senses other than sight. There is something about its whiteness and "purity" that makes the spectator behave in a particular way; there is a tendency to leave more distance between the viewer and the artwork, and very often talking in a whisper as if it were a place of worship.

II.II The emergence of the black box for moving images

In a parallel with the "white box" for viewing artwork images, the "black box" is still held as the paradigm for optimal viewing of moving images. However, a brief look at the history of this artform will show us that it took between twenty and thirty years of evolution for this particular viewing style to establish itself as the singular way of consuming moving images. In the 1920s, there was no single viewing style for film. The "cinema" was wherever the projector was: in a café, an empty garage, under a circus tent, at a fair, or on an improvised vaudeville stage.

Arriving at the dark, anonymous black-box space of most contemporary movie houses took some time, and yet it has persisted. Still today, we associate the movie-going experience with total darkness, separation from the outside world, immobility and silence, and being in a large communal space with other strangers. There is an implicit and socially agreed-upon understanding that as soon as images are projected on the screen, there are certain behavioral norms to follow and a "right way" to experience a movie and behave during its projection, which includes cutting off our senses that are not sight or hearing. How did this ritualistic behavior emerge?

Initially, in trying to find the optimal architectural typology for projecting movies, there was a push to assimilate the design of the first movie houses in the 1920s to established typologies, which derived from Renaissance conceptions of the theater. These conceptions in turn were deeply influenced by the writings of Vitruvius, again based on the optimal proportions of the human body—the unified body—conceived through the universal Vitruvian man. The same geometries of a circle and a square inside it are used in the diagram of theater design to subdivide and organize the space.[11] Renaissance conceptions of architectural organization departed from the idea of man as likened by gods; religion replaced by the human body. It was the humanist unified body, discussed earlier, that permeated most aspects of life in this time period, and materialized in the design of spaces for viewing artwork.

In an attempt to bring the viewing styles of cinema and theater closer together and to elicit equal attention, the first designs of the space for

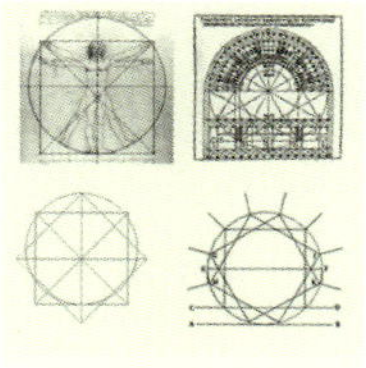

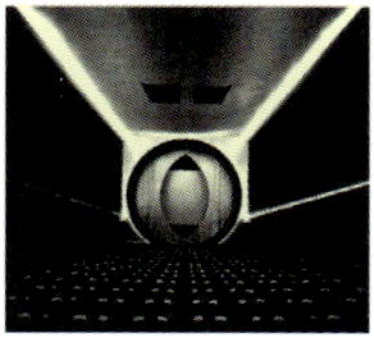

cinema in the early-twentieth century were inspired by Vitruvian notions that permeated the Italian playhouses, which gave rise to the "Vitruvian spectator":[12] someone immersed in the experience of that which is unfolding on the screen, respectful of the physical and communal environment that holds the event, without succumbing to unnecessary distractions.[13] Thus, the physical environment was designed to seem familiar, recall behavioral associations, and instill tight control over the behavior of the spectator.

The assimilation of the Vitruvian theater was fervently questioned by architects, critics, and filmmakers of the mid-twentieth century, who did not agree with using the theater as inspiration for the cinema. Architect Frederick Kiesler pointed to some initial practical reasons for this,[14] but emphasized the uniqueness of the "place" for movies: "the cinema is a play of surfaces, the theatre is a performance in space, and this difference has not yet been translated concretely into any piece of architecture, neither for the theater nor for the cinema."

Unnecessary theatrical elements began to drop away and the assimilation taking place was not about it looking like a theater, but rather affording the same behaviors from the spectator that the theater afforded. Kiesler felt that: "The most important quality of an auditorium for film was the ability to suggest concentrated attention" and, importantly, allowed the spectator to "lose himself in an infinite imaginary space".[15] Kiesler is referencing the physical environment's ability to create a palpable effect on the spectator. As Gabriele Pedullà reminds us, there is an awareness of the psychological effects that particular spatial designs can have over the user, and a "general acknowledgement of the psychological ends of architecture and its ability to control perception".[16]

III Fragmented body | Architecture as an aesthetic device

After decades of aiming to find their place, movies seem to have an established location in the space of the black box. The auditorium's principal objective for the Vitruvian viewer is to impose on the audience a new attitude toward movies, by subjecting spectators to total darkness and voluntarily restricting freedom of movement. Yet, as any contemporary moviegoer knows, cinema is undergoing the same crises that artwork images did once they reached the age of massive reproduction. Given the prevalence of technology that allows the streaming of movies in our own homes, film is now reproducible at the level of the individual, who is able to project a film without the apparatus of the cinema. Thus, the ceremonial quality of the cinema and its uniqueness is now lost.[17] It is no longer enough to just project a movie to entice people. Cinema is poised to find itself a new kind of space.

The appreciation of artworks today is multifaceted and fragmented. Our screens and access to information allow us to have multiple scales of appreciation. We can look at the image of an art piece by zooming into its pixels on a computer or tablet, and also remotely experience the way in which the piece is being displayed by literally panning the globe on our screens to understand its context and physical location in the world. This is fragmentation emerging, not as an opposition to unity, but as repetition of different scales of appreciation, which overlap and juxtapose different information to create a unity of the fragmented. Our appreciation of images is fragmented through repetition and difference yet we can achieve a full understanding of the work of art through these multiple scales available to us.

However, there is still a persistent sensorial distance that these remote modes of appreciation instill. No matter how close we can zoom into an image on our screens, we will not be able to feel the texture of the space where it is hanging, or hear the quiet whispers of fellow visitors in the gallery, or be affected by the myriad environmental and physical factors that distract the spectator of a fresco, where the artwork is fully integrated with the architectural space that houses it. Through physical and digital reproductions, it is possible that we might gain access to aspects of the work that may not be available when visiting in person, but that intangible and yet highly present "aura", which one feels when in direct contact with an artwork image, cannot really be substituted by any device.

There have certainly been attempts to reintroduce this bodily three-dimensional sensorial quality back into the experience of viewing images on screens, in order to make it "more real". The aim to reintroduce the third dimension that was seemingly lost in photography and cinema has sparked the proliferation of 3-D movies or cinema in four dimensions, in an attempt to envelop the spectator in a full-body sensorial experience. Enabled by technology, movie houses are aiming to reinvent the experience with immersive cinema, to make the experience more "real", more three-dimensional.

Paradoxically, with this attempt to provide a more realistic experience, we are constantly reminded of its artificiality. In 3-D movies we are obliged to wear awkward colored glasses to perceive the three-dimensional information. If we were to remove them, nothing but a blurred vision of what is being projected would be perceivable. Thus, in aiming to make the experience more bodily by adding the third dimension of space, we are only able to perceive it through a device that is external to our body, the 3-D glasses. On the other hand, when we are provided with the added sensorial perks of a shivering seat, or a puff of air suddenly blowing in our face, rather than being immersed by the experience, we are reminded of the absurdity of the artifice gone into creating the still awkward effect.

While this 4-D technology is still very much in development, with the advent of the digital in image-making we are undoubtedly in a different place than when images became reproducible via photography or film. It appears that the control is now in the hands of the spectator, able to choose between very different modes of viewership. How can we think about images in the same way now that we are in the post-digital-reproducibility era?

Virtual reality has been one of the new ways to experience images, whether of art, movies or of an entirely different nature, mostly related to gaming. But virtual reality relies on the wearing of devices, usually around the eyes, that shut the physical world out in order to experience an intangible world almost purely through a visual register. The privileging of the visual in virtual reality is exacerbated to such a degree that it denies the multisensorial body that enables us to navigate the world.

Augmented reality does something different. Rather than making us inhabit a reality that is virtual, denying the body, it brings the virtual into our physical world, supposedly augmenting the real. In augmented reality, we are not denying the physicality of our bodies. Instead of trying to mimic the physical environment virtually by shutting off the world, there is a reframing of the physical with the introduction of the virtual: we see the physical anew. To some important degree, it signals a return to the appreciation of the physical environment in which our images found themselves prior to their reproducibility. The images need the physical qualities of the space in order to be understood; there is an interdependence between the space and the virtual image that inhabits that space.

By zooming into moments in history—the Renaissance, the beginning of the twentieth century, and our current condition from the end of the twentieth century onward—we therefore witness a successive distancing from the physical body: going from a united conception of images, body, and space, to a disembodied one separating body and space, to a fragmented one enabled by the pervasiveness of the digital. Built spaces that house artworks, both still and moving images, serve as aesthetic devices to either tightly, or more loosely, control and affect the spectator.

Paradoxically today, while we seem to be in a moment where almost everything can be experienced virtually, the evolution of digital technology is almost nostalgically pointing us back to the times when we depended on our bodies moving through space in order to appreciate the image. With the overabundance of reproduction techniques, enabled by the digital, we are paradoxically returning to the conception of images we had before images could be reproduced with the rapidity that contemporary methods allow. In virtual reality, the device is what controls our experience, by shutting off most of our senses and privileging the visual; while in augmented reality, we are not denying the physicality and the multisensorial quality of our world. Architectural space is still, curiously, the aesthetic device that it was during the Renaissance.

While there is no singular overarching conception of how images are to be experienced today, there certainly is an attempt to regain the loss of dimension implicit in image reproduction, by reintroducing the experiential and sensorial dimension back into the appreciation of art. It seems, however, that the cinema and the art gallery are still in search of a new typology fit for the fragmented spectator.

Endnotes

1 Or kinesthetic sense, also known as proprioception.

2 Not just epitomical examples, like the Sistine Chapel, that clearly need to be experienced in their physical space, but also other pieces, such as the *Mona Lisa*, for instance, that require a physical presence; walking around it, seeing its small stature, commenting on its position on the wall, and the other paintings around it.

3 In the context of this text, drawings and diagrams are considered images.

4 Vitruvius, *The Ten Books of Architecture*, Book Three: *On symmetry*, Translated by Morris Hicky Morgan. London: Humphrey Milford Oxford University Press, p 73.

5 Walter Benjamin. New York: Schocken, 1968, p 220.

6 Gabriele Pedullà, *In Broad Daylight: Movies and Spectators After the Cinema*, New York: Verso, 2012, pp 17–18.

7 Ibid, p 17.

8 It has been reported that 2016 was the worst year for movie income since the 1920s.

9 Pedullà, *In Broad Daylight*, pp 17–18.

10 This is a direct reference to Benjamin's *The Work of Art*. While Benjamin's text is of huge value to the development of the ideas in this text, there is also an understanding of the work of art, which this text moves away from in favor of a multifaceted understanding of how art can be appreciated. "Contrary to what Benjamin thought, there is more than one way to appreciate the work of an architect, to go to the theater, or to look at a painting. If this were not the case, there would be no need for aesthetic devices like the dark cube in the first place." Pedullà, *In Broad Daylight*, p 73.

11 Theater design is covered in Book Five of Vitruvius's text. As Pedullà states: "For Renaissance humanists, educating the public in the classical theater was part of a much more comprehensive project of recreating man in the likeness of the Greek and Romans." *In Broad Daylight*, p 47.

12 This is the title of a chapter in Pedullà's *In Broad Daylight*, pp 37–60.

13 As Gabriele Pedullà recounts, Leon Battista Alberti, in *On the Art of Building in Ten Books*, claimed: "The architect's only task was to put the spectators in a condition to see and hear effortlessly what was happening on stage." *In Broad Daylight*, p 47.

14 For instance: in a movie house, the first rows were no longer the best ones, as in the theater; the side seating provided by elegant boxes also become nonsensical for the viewing of a flat screen which is best viewed frontally; and similarly, the typical fan-shaped seating of the theater house did not provide the best view for the flat screen.

15 Frederick Kiesler quoted in Pedullà, *In Broad Daylight*, pp 51–52.

16 Certainly, the shift in the type of space was also enabled by movies that required more attention, and based on narration. However, they could not have emerged without a concerted effort to control the viewer's perception of space through the careful design and associative power that physical space has on the subject, and its capacity to appreciate the object. To quote Pedullà further: "Imitating the theater, the dark cube in fact aspired to propose itself as a place of absolute aesthetic experience that allowed only one legitimate activity: the contemplation of a film. [...]

Suddenly, going to the movies was like going to church." *In Broad Daylight*, p 33.

17 The aura that Benjamin refers to when discussing art, although, according to him, film did not have aura at all.

Bibliography

Alberti, Leon Battista. *On the Art of Building in Ten Books*. Cambridge, MA: MIT Press, 1988.

Benjamin, Walter. "The Work of Art in the Age of Mechanical Reproduction", in *Illuminations*. New York: Schocken, 1968.

Coccia, Emanuele. *The Sensible Life*. New York: Fordham University Press, 2016.

Freud, Sigmund. *Civilization and its Discontents*. Translated by James Strachey. New York: W.W. Norton & Company, Inc, 1961.

Freud, Sigmund. "The Uncanny" in *The Standard Edition of the Complete Psychological Works of Sigmund Freud*, vol XVII (1919): *An Infantile Neurosis and Other Works*, pp 217–256.

Kagis McEwen, Inga. *Vitruvius. Writing the Body of Architecture*. Cambridge, MA: MIT Press, 2003.

Lacan, Jacques. "The Direction of the Treatment and the Principles of its Power" in *Écrit: A Selection*. New York: Norton, 1977, pp 250–310.

Paleotti, Gabriele. *Discourse on Sacred and Profane Images*. Los Angeles: Getty Publications, 2012.

Pedullà, Gabriele. *In Broad Daylight: Movies and Spectators After the Cinema*. New York: Verso, 2012.

Phillips, Stephen J. *Elastic Architecture: Frederick Kiesler and Design Research in the First Age of Robotic Culture*. Cambridge: MIT Press, 2017.

Vitruvius. *The Ten Books on Architecture.* Translated by Morris Hicky Morgan. London: Humphrey Milford Oxford University Press, 1914.

Vitruvius. *The Architecture of M. Vitruvius, Pollio*. Translated by W. Newton, vol 1. London: Creative Media Partners, LLC, 1791.

Illustrations

Vitruvian Man, p 12. https://www.leonardodavinci.net/the-vitruvian-man.jsp.

Francesco di Giorgio Martini, p 13. *Drawing for a Church*. Original source: Scanned from The Evolution of Designs: Biological Analogy in Architecture and the Applied Arts by Philip Steadman, found in https://leonardodavinci.stanford.edu/submissions/clabaugh/history/architecture.html.

Sketches of the evolution of artwork display spaces, p 15. By author.

Black box evolution sketches, p 16. By author.

Vitruvian Man and Theater Plan, p 17. https://politicworm.files.wordpress.com/2009/11/ground-plan-ces1.jpg.

Italian playhouse theater, p 17. http://www3.northern.edu/wild/th100/Olimpico2.jpg.

Film Guild Cinema by Frederick Kiesler, p 17. Found in http://cinematreasures.org/theaters/4699.

Freud's study desk at Berggasse 19, p 17. Found in The Emergence of The Interior: Architecture, Modernity, Domesticity, p 43.

choreographing space

Choreographing Space was created as an exploration into the overlaps of space, movement, art, and performance with public engagement. In the years following 9/11, downtown Manhattan became a ghost town; stores went out of business, those who could found housing in less toxic areas, and the community was left stranded. This project was one of the efforts to revitalize downtown after the trauma by bringing public art to the community. We were awarded a grant to support our work in an abandoned storefront space, our first design-build installation to bring together Eva's professional dance training and Ian's lifelong skateboarding with an extraordinary group of emerging artists in dance choreography, music composition, costume design, and dance filmmaking.

Our goal was to engage the public and explore how the design of spaces influences the way we move, behave, and act. Space-making is not an innocent act, it has the power to affect those who are in it—it has consequences. Like choreography, the spaces of our built environment are significantly concerned with the movement of people through them, yet they have historically been conceived of and materialized through static organizational models that deal more with the idea of permanence, stability, and privilege rather than the welcoming movement of all kinds of bodies within it. Choreographing Space is a project that aimed to challenge inert models of organization in order to provide a public refuge in challenging times, an approach to art that is welcoming and inclusive, oscillating between being a container for art and being art itself.

Inspired by catenary structures—a form defined by the curvature of naturally suspended chains—we enveloped the interior of the storefront space with an interactive mesh capable of transformation and made from off-the-shelf wiffle balls and many hours of experimentation. The project became at once a performance event and an architectural environment, fusing performer and audience, space and movement.

The space opened to the public as a relaxing, meditative, yet interactive environment during the day, when visitors were also invited to "play" the space. It transformed into a performance space in the evenings with uniquely curated weekly events: starting with a dance-film screening, followed by live performances with sound pieces written specifically for each show. The space was activated by the movement of the performers flowing along the floor topography, weaving through the audience and manipulating the suspended mesh into a continuously changing environment.

interactive
mesh nodes
string mesh
stepped floor
topography
installation within
the existing space

Choreographing Space was a beautiful project. I still recall, many years later, the soft white curvilinear motion of the installation and floor space both intersecting out over the audience and to the opposite wall. It was vital for me to be part of an artistic project in response to the 9/11 tragedy in NYC. As a first-hand witness of this horrible event, I needed to heal and help others heal in my community. The storefronts downtown were vacant for years and it was wonderful to be part of the transformation of space with our bodies in the context of art and architecture. Eva and Ian's vision of reimagining the space inspired me to structure a site-specific dance. I brought in three female artists, who contributed their own ideas to the dance. The dancers and I worked in harmony with the installation dancing to a new composition by composer Alex Davis.

It was indeed meditative and peaceful.

Kim Jones, choreographer and artistic director of Movement Migration

Project data

- **Location** Lower Manhattan, New York City
- **Design and fabrication** Eva Perez de Vega + Ian Gordon
- **Fabrication assistants** Pablo Baquero, Flavia Bertorello, Merily Jurna, Eva Perrotta and Jennifer Riggi
- **Choreography and dance** Nya Bowman, Veruska Cantelli, Esther Eiras, Saskia Hannemann, Kim Jones, Stacey Kaplan, Eva Perez de Vega, Eva Perrotta, Liz Ross, Yana Schnitzler, Kristina Skjelberg, Kristina Skovby and Maia Sørensen
- **Music composers** Robert Boston, Alex Davis, Jean-Philippe Feiss, April Koester and David Potaux-Razel
- **Costume design** Atsuko Yagi
- **Dance short films** *No One* by Arielle Javitch and *Nude* by Maia Sørensen
- **Photography** Julieta Cervantes and Brandon Jacobs-Mills
- **Public events curator:** Eva Perez de Vega
- **Organizations:** made possible by a grant from the Lower Manhattan Cultural Council generously supported by The September 11th Fund

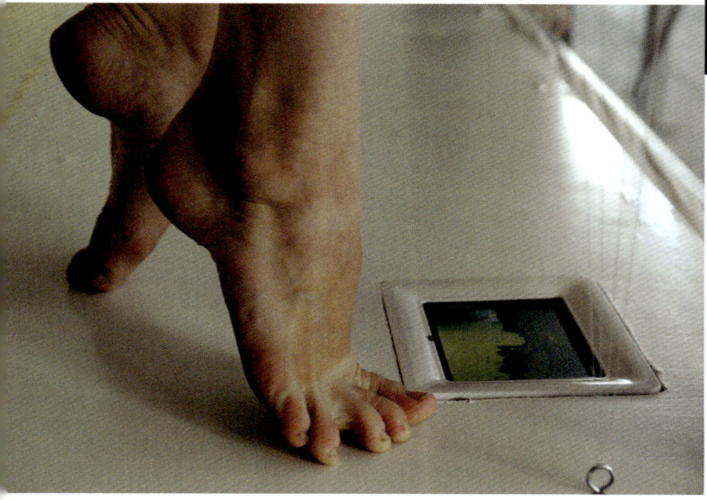

Strada Dinamica is the second pavilion we designed for our cross-continent client Ceramics of Italy, promoter of Italian ceramics and culture. After our five-year working relationship on the first pavilion, the client did something unprecedented in their history by hiring the same architects to build a second pavilion for their largest yearly event opening in Chicago. The brief was similar but the goals were different: the pavilion needed to be welcoming but not foster long-term gathering. Therefore, it became a lively Italian streetscape that favors movement and dynamic interactions over stationary gatherings. Visitors are invited to flow through the space from multiple directions and funnel into emergent patterns within zones for coffee, aperitivo, seating, and quick meals around communal tables. These long, interlocking, and reconfigurable elements help create the dynamic, winding streetscape while providing welcoming dining surfaces or "tablescape".

The large-scale expo that this pavilion is part of usually generates an incredible amount of waste. We aimed to work against this tendency by encouraging an efficient usage of materials; designing all the elements of the pavilion, including the ceramic tile that covered most surfaces, to be reused for several years and upcycled at the end. To that end, the floor was made up of a novel floating-floor system that allowed the full recuperation and reuse of the material.

The project embodies a sense of flow that is emphasized through the use of horizontal lines of sight and a striated design across all elements. This effect is materialized by a lower structure of grooved, curved wooden panels for the kiosks and a similarly striated overhanging canopy made up of a lightweight stretched fabric over a curved metallic structure. The tile tonality for the floor is reminiscent of Roman travertine. The color palette is intentionally limited to white and brown to accentuate the lines of sight and a sense of flow created by the sculptural forms. The only exception is the info-totem that acts as a clear landmark within the larger expo, standing out with its vibrant Italian colors.

As this pavilion is situated in a central location within the Italian expo, proximity to it is very sought-after by other stands, which strategize for months prior to opening. The pavilion becomes a political object of some contention, but is also seen as an art object itself: a spatial manifestation of the culture it showcases.

eramics of Italy

Project data

- **Location** Chicago
- **Design** Eva Perez de Vega + Ian Gordon
- **Organization** Ceramics of Italy
- **Offsite Fabrication** A&M Production
- **Onsite Assembly** Freeman

Ceramics of Italy

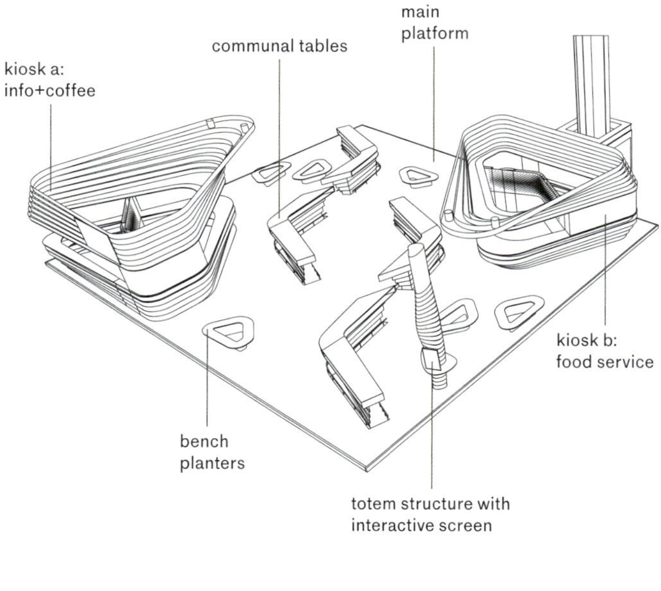
main
platform
communal tables
kiosk a:
info+coffee
kiosk b:
food service
bench
planters
totem structure with
interactive screen

jeongok prehistory museum

2006

As a response to an international competition, this was one of the early projects, before e+i was officially formed. It is part of a series of projects that anticipates interests we continued to develop in our collaboration as e+i studio.

The design for the Gyeonggi-do Jeongok Prehistory Museum emerged from an awareness of the natural flows through the site that connect the existing facilities of the Paleolithic Excavation Site, the Prehistoric Park, the History Cultural Village and Hantan River, without interfering with the topographical condition by bridging over layers of history above the crevice of excavation. Thus, the proposed museum structures are quite literally a materialization of those flows, intensifying them at specific moments with program and structure.

The identification of the basalt precipice as a crucial and central component to the design suggested the possibility of bridge-like structures that would have the dual function of allowing views from above the basalt crevice while minimizing any disturbance to the site and its geology. Furthermore, a bridge structure allows a certain elevation above ground, thus permitting excellent views of the natural surroundings without the need of any additional structures. Thus, the museum structures are two intersecting bridges of poured concrete, structurally working as one.

The north-south building invites visitors and employees into the facilities from the south side and is anchored into the landscape on the north, opening onto a garden and leisure spaces. The welcoming accessible ramps follow the natural slope of the site until they bifurcate into two volumes: the lower one contains all the private staff programs while the upper volume holds the public areas (lobby, café and store). The east-west building is a bridge structure that contains the main exhibition spaces as well as the educational programs. This volume is connected to the north-south structure at the lobby, by means of a curved enclosed ramp, from which one can enjoy the striking views of the site environment and basalt crevice.

Our proposal for Jeongok's Prehistory Museum combines architecture and landform into a codependent viewing experience that explores prehistory beyond textual historicity. The geological layers of the crevice become a display of work, revealing themselves as an artform in their own right.

site plan

01 prehistory park
02 pedestrian paths
03 outdoor events space
04 world's oldest plant garden (ginko tree, metasequoia...)
05 aromatic plantings + seasonal flowers
06 flower and tea garden
07 outdoor seating and landscaped area
08 colored gravel and earth with natural dyes
09 car and bus parking
10 evergreen trees
11 basalt precipice glazed enclosure
12 excavation site jeongok-ri paleolithic site
13 lookout spot: viewing of excavation site
14 lookout spot: view of hantan river
15 recreation digs for children

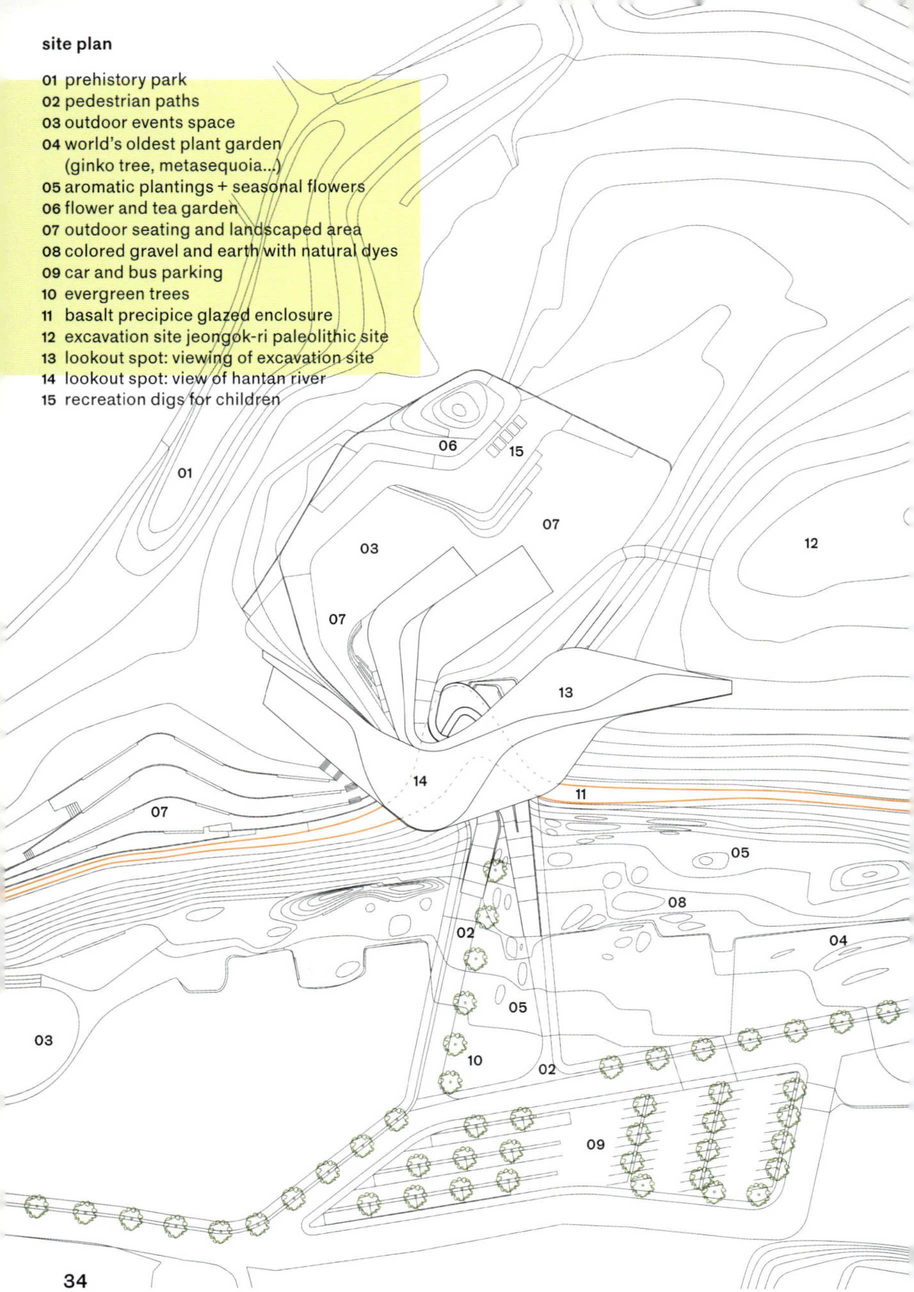

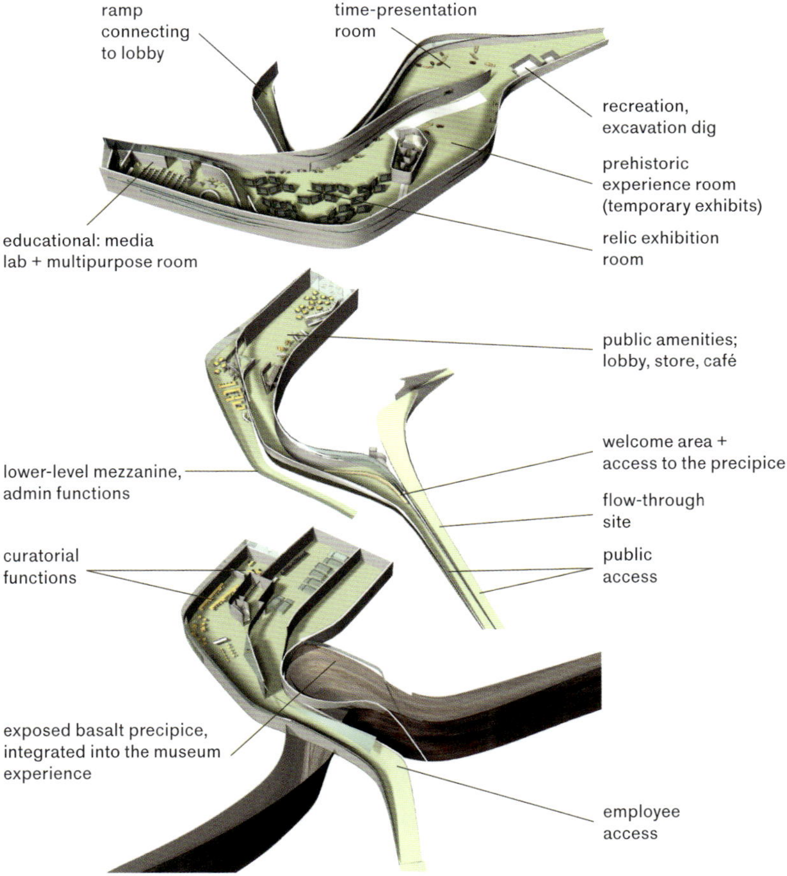

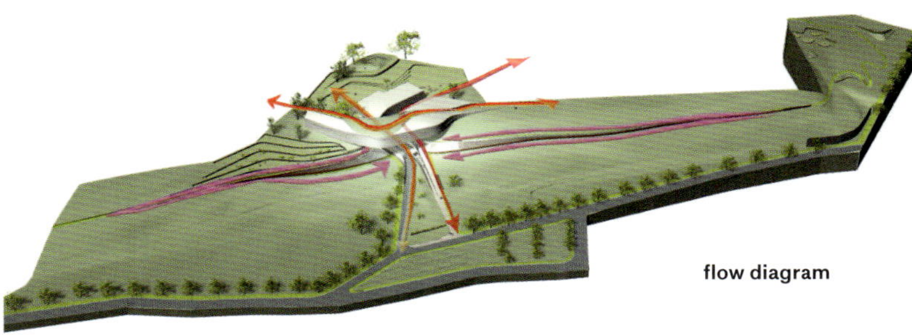

flow diagram

Project data

- **Location** Jeongok, Gyeonggi-do, South Korea
- **Design** Eva Perez de Vega
- **Organization** Gyeonggi Provincial Government

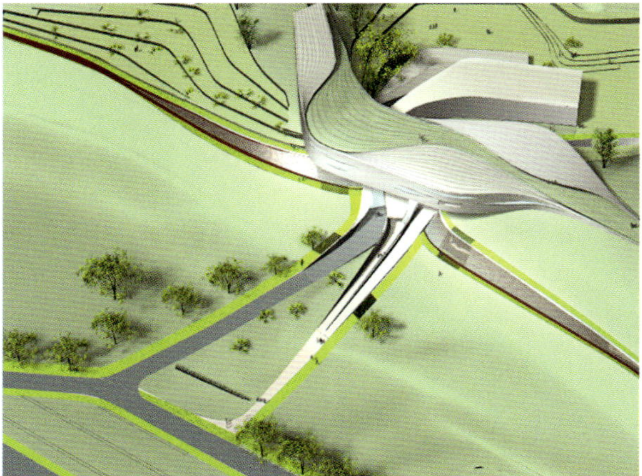

eyewear showroom

2013

This pop-up eyewear store— a collaboration between fashion and architecture for a high-end eyewear designer—was designed to be inside a shipping container and deployed on Pier 57 overlooking the Hudson River during a summer festival. The project proposes a series of clustered columns that serve as spatial display elements, made up of a series of modular units, which are themselves the eyewear display as well as the eyewear cases. These units stacked in varying ways create column-like elements that are strategically clustered to direct the user flow, inviting meandering and a break from the rigid banality of the rectangular shipping container.

To address the wastefulness typical of temporary structures, we designed these column-like elements to become remnants themselves as each display unit becomes the eyewear case for the buying customer. With every eyewear purchase, one stacked module would disappear, so that, for the duration of the summer festival, the columns would get smaller before totally disappearing at the closing. The uncanny anthropomorphic scale of the columns invites viewers to approach and interact with the context, in a similar way that one may explore and roam through the remnant columns of a Roman forum.

The freestanding column elements on the exterior suggest continuity between the inside and the exterior and serve as visual markers that locate the installation on an urban scale. Clustered seating areas allow for pauses within the space to try the eyewear, socialize, and appreciate the design objects within the manufactured landscape of the architectural proposal.

The gallery is understood as a temporary and flexible setting for the display of eyewear products, hinging between product and artwork. Reflecting on the ephemerality of fashion seasons, the architecture itself disappears before the season is over.

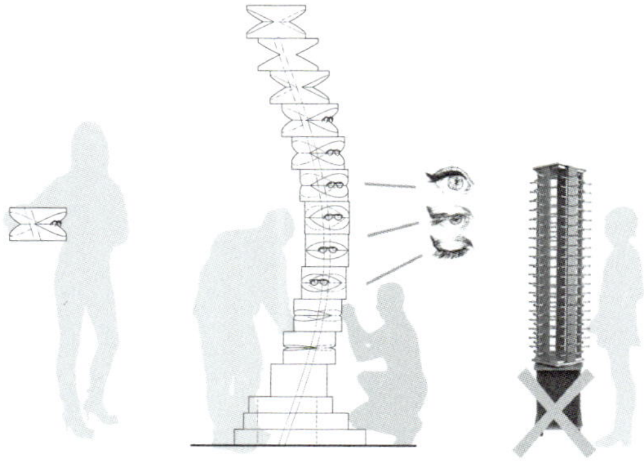

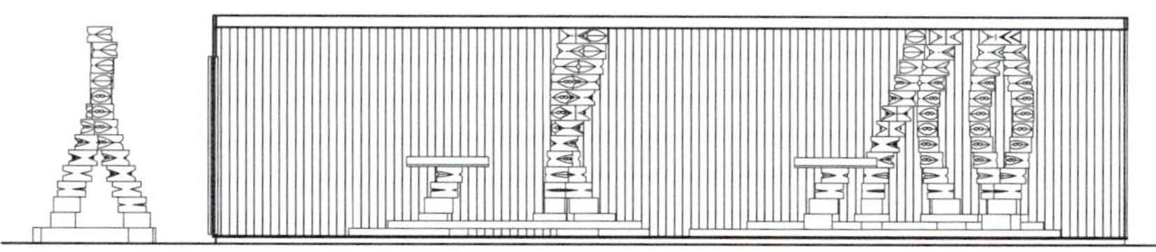

longitudinal section

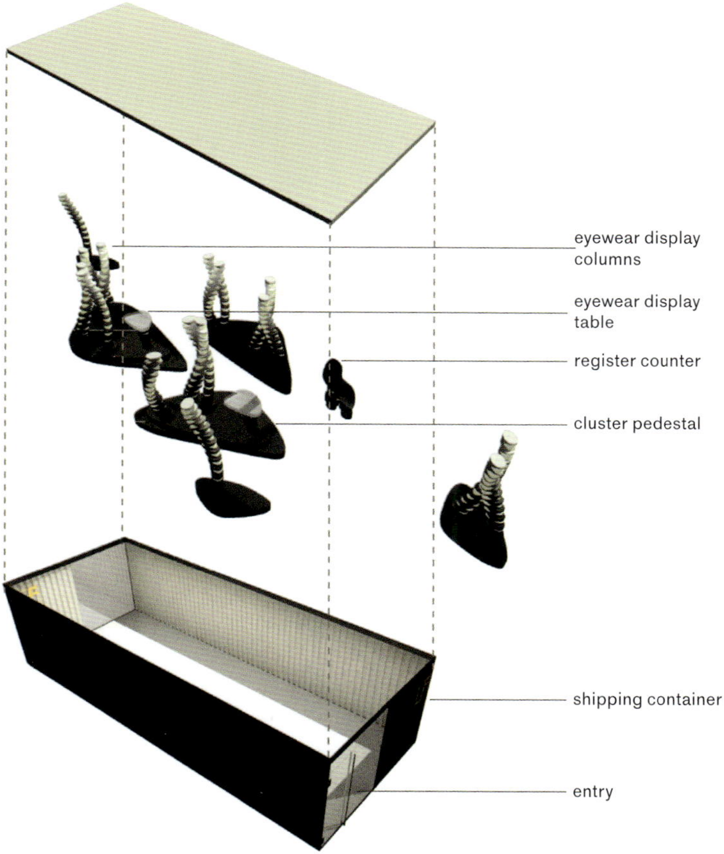
eyewear display columns
eyewear display table
register counter
cluster pedestal
shipping container
entry

Project data

- **Location** Pier 57, New York City
- **Design** Eva Perez de Vega + Ian Gordon
- **Posthuman render** Ziyu Chen
- **Organization** BOFFO, non-profit arts and culture organization

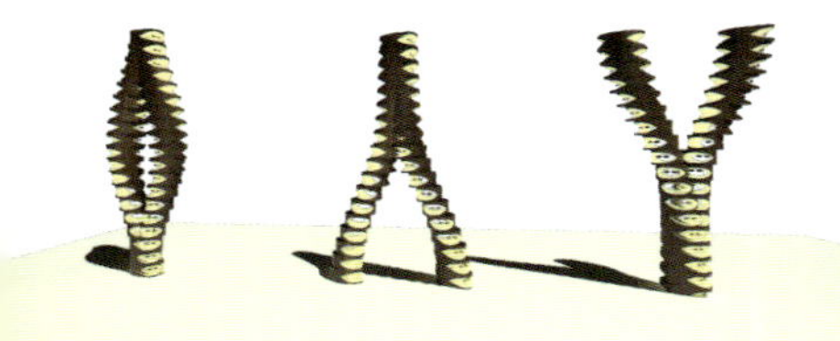

OPPOSITE If left on the pier, without excessive human intervention, the project would most likely become engulfed with vegetation, thriving with the return of local New York plants and a burgeoning of Karner blue and monarch butterflies, cottontail and migratory birds.

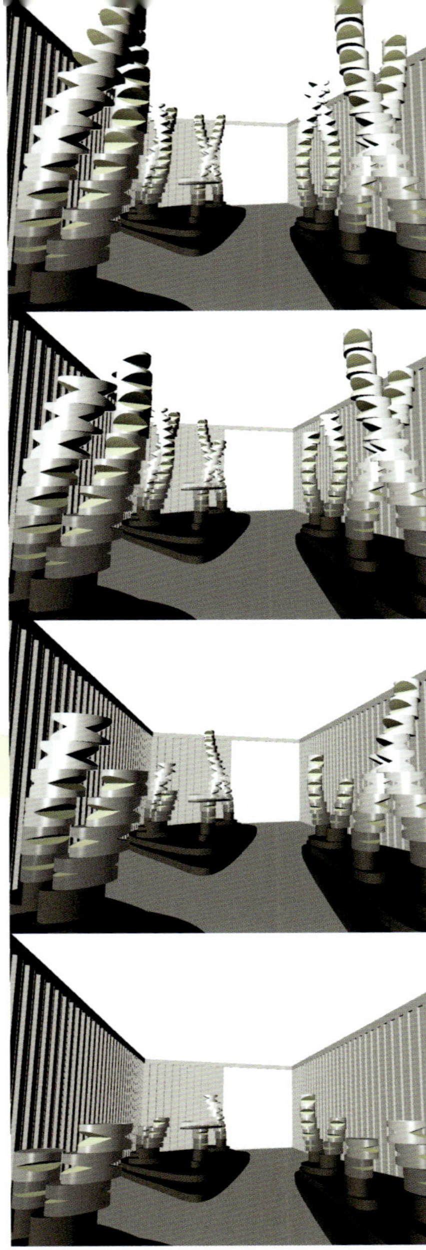

evolution of showroom over time

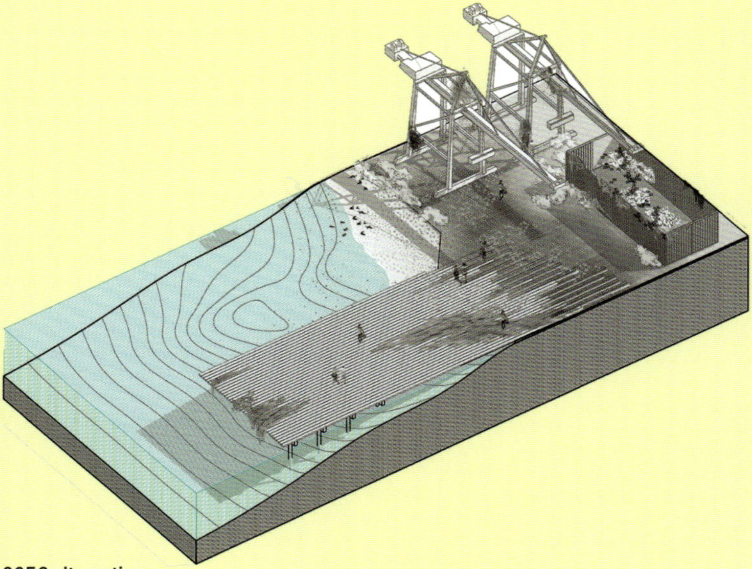

2050 alternative

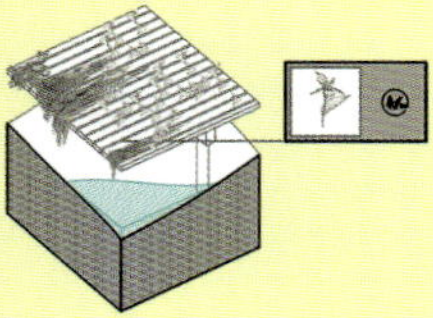

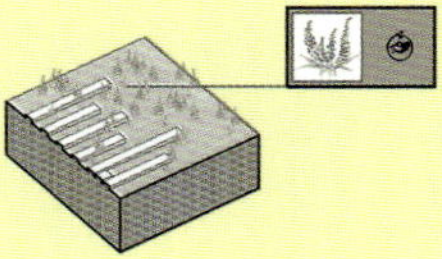

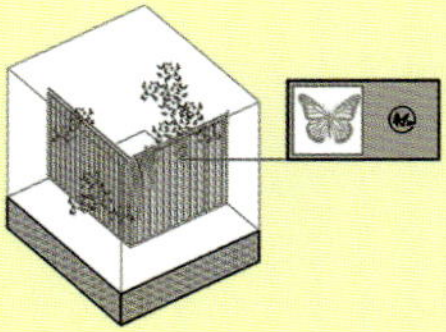

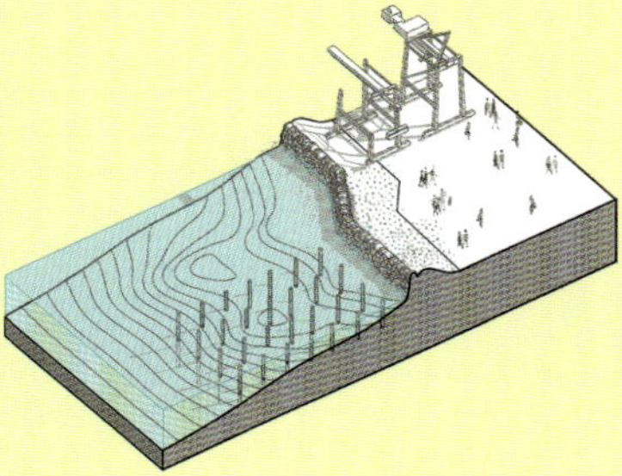

2050

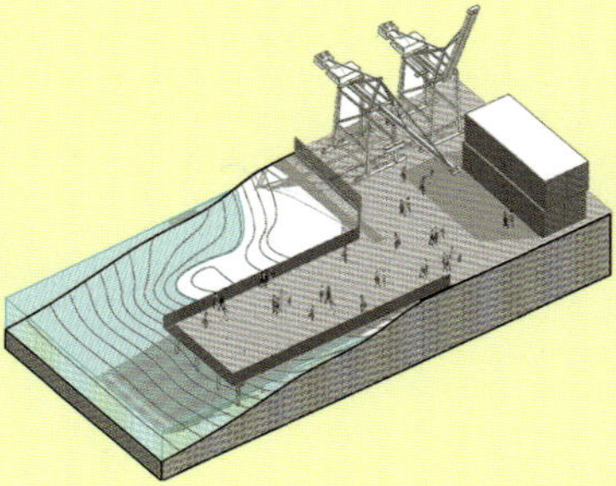

present

engage

I Fusion and regression

If we think of architecture as the formation of material and geometry experienced through our bodily sensations, and psychoanalysis as the exploration of the inner psyche, one would wonder what these two disciplines might contribute to one another. The experience of architecture—our built, physical reality—is not limited to our external physical body, just as psychoanalysis is not limited to the inner world of the mind. Instead, there is an ongoing dialogue, where the physical environment—consciously or unconsciously—has an effect on the psyche, which simultaneously affects one's perception of that physical reality. As such, buildings do not merely provide physical shelter and protection, they also provide a mental mediation between the world and our consciousness, articulating both physical and existential space.

In his writings, Sigmund Freud gives little insight into the nature of the physical space; the furniture and numerous objects he surrounds himself and his patients with during sessions. However, in looking at how the spatial setting of a psychoanalyst's office might affect the outcome of a session, one can attempt to determine the role of the space of analysis—the use of the couch, the controlled visual, auditory, and tactile environment. It acts as a catalyst to simultaneously disorient and orient, confuse and enlighten, frighten and shelter the patient; to evoke simultaneous—yet not contradictory—opposing "uncanny"[1] sensations, which extract the patient from his or her particular perspective of reality and reorient them into a state of fusion with the space itself. This can be compared to experiencing a work of art, where one becomes fused with the object of observation. It is also not dissimilar from Freud's notion of "oceanic feeling",[2] associated with the baby's contentment during breastfeeding.

I.I Fusion with the object of observation

Freud first refers to the "oceanic feeling" in the opening pages of *Civilization and its Discontents*, in the context of letters exchanged with his friend, now known to be French writer Romain Rolland: "It is a feeling which he would like to call a sensation of 'eternity', a feeling as of something limitless, unbounded—as it were, 'oceanic'."[3]

Considering himself a man of science, Freud analyzes the term as he would any other feeling, namely by exploring what causes it, or as he put it, he sets out to find its "ideational content".[4] Tracing it back to the early phase of ego-feeling, or primary narcissism, Freud explains that our present ego-feeling is only a reduced fragment of an earlier, more encompassing feeling, in which the ego and the outside world are intimately bound. The ideational content of this primitive ego is precisely that of limitlessness and of a bondage with the universe; the same ideas that characterize the "oceanic feeling".

This state of indissoluble bond, of oneness with the universe, is what Freud associated with the baby's contentment during breastfeeding. For Freud, the primary ego-feeling coexists, as a kind of counterpart, to the narrower and more sharply demarcated ego-feeling of maturity, and compares this ego to the vestiges of ancient Rome lying beneath the constructions of later centuries.[5] In a different—yet similar—conception, for psychoanalyst Donald Winnicott, the infant is a mind-body entity unaware of its separation from the environment, from its mother.[6] At the same time the illusion of oneness in maturity is a necessary phase in the recognition of the state of separateness, of differentiation between self and other.[7] From either one of these vantages the question that necessarily arises is: what triggers this "oceanic feeling" in maturity?[8]

There have been many accounts by artists who, when describing the creative act, speak of a loss of self and a sense of fusion with the object of creation; "art is made at the boundary between self and the world".[9] However, artistic experience can also be extended to the viewing of a work of art. In his book *The Power of Form*, psychoanalyst Gilbert Rose describes the aesthetic experience of viewing art as "a sense of fusion with the art work. Subject, object, and interaction become interwoven in a dynamic system."[10]

When observing becomes a creative act itself, it is an immersive experience that weakens the boundary between self and object of observation; the borderline softens, turns permeable, and allows the world to flow into the viewer and the viewer to flow into the world. This state of oneness corresponds to a state of indeterminacy of boundaries, which seems to be the same as that described by Freud with the "oceanic feeling".[11] It also coincides with Winnicott's conception of the intermediary state of experiencing; in which the inner and the outer world of a human being coexist in an interrelated yet separate way, limited only by a porous "membrane".[12] Thus, instead of passive reception followed by an outward reaction in an immersive aesthetic experience, we become an open dynamic system where self and world are embodied in each other.

According to Rose in *The Power of Form*, although the sense of fusion with artwork is quite different to that of the original narcissistic fusion of self with the mother (in that there is no genetic source for this experience) this "inner unity unconsciously echoes the original oneness with the mother".[13] Rose also sustains that aesthetic fusion is temporary and followed by the idea of re-separation; the dissolution of boundaries is followed by their re-delineation. He goes on to discuss the experience of aesthetic fusion as involving an oscillatory, pendulum-like movement between past and present, fantasy and reality, with the artwork acting as a "transitional bridge between the strange and the familiar".[14] When tackling this idea in the context of physical space he finds that it is "both enveloping, embracing, inclusive and delineating, segregating, exclusive".[15]

Similarly, the art critic Adrian Stokes—whose writings were heavily influenced by psychoanalytic theory in general, and Kleinian theory in particular—saw in aesthetic experience the integration of the prototypical experiences of fusion and separation of a child with the mother.[16] Stokes writes that any creative act comprises at once a wish for fusion with the object, an "oceanic" longing for it, but also recognition of the otherness of the object. Thus, observing artwork in an immersive way has the capacity to place ourselves at the boundary surface between the real and the imaginary, the outer and the inner, allowing both to flow in and through, just as described by Winnicott as a membrane limiting inside and outside.

In psychoanalysis, when the patient feels stimulated enough to settle in the space, there is potential for an aesthetic experience, for a diffusion of boundaries in such a way that the separation between the patient and the space of analysis softens, while still maintaining an awareness of the otherness of the space. The fusion of self with space brings the patient back to when it was not possible to distinguish between self and the outside world, where fantasy and fiction, body and mind were a single entity, thus pushing the patient into a state of regression. In Winnicott's words:

> *The setting of analysis reproduces the early and earliest mothering techniques. It invites regression by reason of its reliability. The regression of a patient is an organized return to early dependence or double dependence. The patient and the setting merge into the original success situation of primary narcissism.*[17]

Thus, regression is stimulated by a sense of oneness, or fusion, with the environment. In the aesthetic experience—as accounted by Rose and Stokes among others—it is the internal oscillatory movement between opposing sensations that triggers a sense of oneness with the object of observation. Can a parallel be made within the setting of psychoanalysis?

I.II The uncanny

The notion of fusion discussed here coincides in part with Winnicott's intermediate state of experiencing; where inner and outer reality constantly permeate each other, but it is brought about by an internal oscillatory movement. This movement is much like the way electricity is brought about in an alternating current circuit; oscillating from one pole to the other in a consistent and imperceptible way.[18] What produces electricity is the very movement from one to the other—neither positive nor negative charges are ever experienced in their individual state, and electric current needs both polarities in order to exist. In other words, it is a new state that is brought about by the rapid and oscillatory movement between opposing states.

To justify a comparison between fusion triggered by observing artwork and fusion triggered in the context of a psychoanalytic session, one must turn to the concept of "the uncanny", as first developed by Freud in his 1919 paper of the same name. Freud's paper, "Unheimlich" literally meaning unhomely but translated into English as "The Uncanny",[19] deals with the notion of domesticity and familiarity, putting forward the circumstances in which the familiar can become uncanny and frightening. Freud explores the psychodynamics of that which arouses dread and horror, and is particularly interested in the duality inherent in the meaning of the term:[20]

> *In general we are reminded that the word "heimlich" [homelike] is not unambiguous, but belongs to two sets of ideas, which, without being contradictory, are yet very different: on the one hand it means what is familiar and agreeable, and on the other, what is concealed and kept out of sight.*[21]

It is through the concept of the uncanny that psychology has entered most eloquently into the discourse of architecture. In broad strokes, architecture of the uncanny is one that organizes form and space in such a way as to produce unsettling and ambivalent sensations, oscillating between the familiar and the unfamiliar, the alien and the safe, the *unheimlich* and the *heimlich*. Anthony Vidler,[22] who was the first to coin the term "the architectural uncanny", in his book of the same title, uses the uncanny as a metaphor for a fundamentally "unhomely" modern condition and argues that in architecture, the uncanny can be found in the interstices between the psyche and dwelling, between body and space, between the unconscious and its habitat.[23]

Thus, the spatial quality of the analyst's consulting room has a significant role in instigating the sense of fusion necessary for regression. Its uncanny quality of familiarity and strangeness, its embodiment of comfort and discomfort, brings about an internal movement—oscillating from positive to negative—that momentarily fuses the patient with the environment. The space of analysis becomes at once container and content, a modeling and a carving of the subconscious.[24]

II The analyst's office as the uncanny

Freud never really discussed in any detail the relevance of the physical space of analysis in the process or outcome of psychoanalytic treatment. It was probably Winnicott who first tackled this theme in his 1954 paper, "Metapsychological and Clinical Aspects of Regression within the Psycho-Analytical Set-Up". According to Winnicott, the place of regression had not really been given much importance or space for debate within the world of psychoanalysis, and when it did come up, it was often dismissed as pertaining to an "art aspect of psycho-analytic practice".[25]

In describing the setting of Freud's work, Winnicott writes a passage that is key because it intends to explore the impact the physical milieu has on the psyche during the process of analysis:

> *Now I wish to make clear in what way I artificially divide Freud's work into two parts. First, there is the technique of psycho-analysis [...] second, there is the setting in which this work is carried through. [...] This work was done in a room, not a passage, a room that was quiet and not liable to sudden and unpredictable sounds [hearing], yet not dead quiet and not free from ordinary house noises. This room would be lit properly [sight], but not by a light staring in the face, and not by a variable light. The room would certainly not be dark and it would be comfortably warm. The patient would be lying on a couch [touch], that is to say comfortable, if able to be comfortable, and probably a rug and some water would be available [taste].*[26]

It is of interest that in this short but detailed passage about the analyst's room, Winnicott makes reference to bodily sensations through the conventional human senses.[27] No reference is made to smell,[28] which is an interesting absence since Freud actually equated an inability to smell as a means for our consciousness to repress unwanted memories:

> *To put it crudely, the current memory stinks just as an actual object stinks; and just as we turn away our sense organ (the head and nose) in disgust, so do our preconsciousness and our conscious sense turn away from the memory. This is repression.*[29]

II.I The room's thresholds

The first emphasis Winnicott places is on the non-transient quality of the room. Indeed, in entering the analyst's office, both the patient and the analyst know that something very particular is supposed to happen in that space; it is like the stage for an unscripted unfolding of the unconscious; for a radical transformation of self. In theory, successful treatment would entail a somewhat conventional structure of a narrative with a beginning (first encounter with analyst, exchange of formalities), a middle (the routine sessions), and an end (final unfolding of the unconscious, the cure), which is paralleled by the sequence of arrival, with the thresholds anticipating the beginning of treatment or the beginning of that day's session. The sequence of arrival contains multiple thresholds; subtle and powerful elements in establishing the dialectic between inside and outside. The building lobby, stairs, elevator, reception, and waiting room are just some of the possible sequential spaces traversed prior to arriving. As one enters the building's precinct and proceeds toward the analytic room, layers of space are penetrated; preparing for the inner transformation, and insulating patient and analyst from the outside world.

A threshold is the intersection of different spaces, yet it is a space itself, defining both separation and connection. It can be a literal boundary, with visible presence, or just an implied boundary, defined by a ray of light, a scent, a change in material, a piece of furniture, or space between objects—like the distance from a chair to the couch.[30] Nonetheless, thresholds are fiercely felt both physically and emotionally. In entering the space of analysis, the role of a threshold is that of a connector and separator of the outside world; mediating oneness and separateness.

It is not only through the visible spectrum that we can locate or reorient ourselves within the context of space; the auditory canal can also help us understand the non-visible depth of the space, allowing us to perceive the existence of spaces beyond what our eyes may reach. Differently shaped rooms, materials, and textures reverberate sound differently. As such, sound can measure quality as well as quantity of space, making its scale comprehensible; "We stroke the edges of the space with our ears."[31]

In referencing sound when describing the analyst's setting, Winnicott brings domesticity into this otherwise professional setting, implying that somehow ordinary house noises might be the familiar background, which could give the patient a certain comfort. Indeed, comfort seems to be the prevailing quality that, according to Winnicott, the analyst aims to provide. Winnicott's mention of domesticity is worth noting, as it points to the very domesticity in which Freudian discourse of psychoanalysis is produced. Indeed, Freud's consultation rooms, both in Vienna and later in London, were adjacent to the domestic spaces he shared with his family. Domestic sounds were thus likely to have been an indirect part of his sessions with patients.

Yet another threshold is offered by the presence of the window in the consulting room. It mediates the interior and the exterior, providing both a view to the outside world and a reflective surface, which, at a given moment, may reflect back our sense of self. If the window is very large, we can imagine there being more of the outside in the room than the inside, and it could also be a cause for distraction. Too small an opening, however, might have a claustrophobic effect on the patient, and cause a feeling of imprisonment from which one would want to escape. One could make a parallel between the role of the window and the analyst as both being mediators of inside and outside, and also capable, at the necessary moment, of providing a reflection of self to the patient.

II.II The couch

Although Freud does not enter into details of the spatial organization of the analytic setting, he does provide reasons for the use of the couch and the position of the analyst behind the reclined patient. The first motive was personal; he did not wish to be looked at for long periods of time, but on the professional level, he wrote that he did not want to give the patient any material for interpretation by reading the analyst's facial expressions:

I insist on this procedure, however, for its purpose and result are to prevent the transference from mingling with the patient's associations imperceptibly, to isolate the transference and to allow it to come forward in due course sharply defined as a resistance.[32]

Indeed, one of the most common images associated with the process of psychoanalysis is the patient lying on the clinician's couch. The couch as an object within the spatial setting of the analyst's consulting room is heavily embedded with meaning; its physical presence is powerful not merely due to its size, but because it is intimately related to the process of regression and personal transformation. Freud used the couch as a tool to encourage regression; to accompany the journey into the unconscious and recovery of the repressed. Analysts after Freud have long recognized that the positioning of the patient on the couch facilitates regression to earlier modes of psychic organization, in part because the recumbent position resembles the position of sleep. In describing the analytical setting, psychoanalyst René Spitz claimed that with the use of the couch and free association Freud had created a surprising parallel to the infantile situation:

The couch on which the patient lies in the infantile situation, without seeing, but hearing the analyst, having to address his appeals and expressive manifestations into the emptiness of space like the infant.[33]

However, from the patient's point of view, there is also something very alienating and disorienting about being in a semi-horizontal position within the relatively foreign environment which is the analyst's office. This ungrounded position implies a certain instability—a shift from being upright, mobile, and physically in control to being passive, and in a state of suspension and induced self-observation. Philosopher Gaston Bachelard uses the term "immensity" to reference the loss of boundaries, which corresponds to the daydreaming state:

As soon as we become motionless, we are elsewhere; we are dreaming in a world that is immense. Indeed, immensity is the movement of motionless man. It is one of the characteristics of quiet daydreaming.[34]

Although there is passivity to being in this state of suspension, it is with the shift from grounded to ungrounded that the perspective of the room shifts; it changes the room from being a mere container of static objects to a palpitating space fully participant in the dynamic transformation of self. In effect, by completely reorienting the patient physically, there is also a reorientation of mental space.

This Freudian radical change in orientation, reorientation or reversal of space, was coined by Lacan's use of the term "anamorphosis".[35] Used in reference to the viewing of art, anamorphosis implies a distortion of perspective,

requiring the viewer to change vantage point or use other mechanisms in order to understand that which is being looked at.[36] An eloquent example is Hans Holbein's hidden depiction of a skull in the painting *The Ambassadors*. When we look at the painting in a direct, frontal way, the skull appears as a meaningless stain, only acquiring the contours of the known object when we change our position and look at it from the side. This notion of anamorphosis also ties back quite strongly to Freud's thoughts on the baby's first turn from the frontal, always available, view of the breast to the profile view which satisfies only imaginarily and allows for normal development in the baby.[37] Psychoanalyst James Grotstein also pointed out how, by recommending analysts place patients on the couch, Freud had in effect discovered the right side of the brain; shifting the patient from a highly organized mode of thinking, now associated with the left brain, to the free-floating, field-dependent right side of the brain.[38]

Psychoanalyst George Moraitis provides another interesting interpretation of Freud's use of the couch; equating it to a protective shield for the analyst whose private space becomes invaded by the patient's transference expectations. In his view, the patient's horizontal position gives the analyst a protective shield that prevents the premature disclosure of the analyst's limitations and vulnerabilities as they emerge in the analytic situation. When the use of the couch is viewed in the light of these considerations, the frequently encountered reluctance of patients to use the couch may indicate an effort to remove the analyst's protective shield; "The use of the couch has traditionally provided the psychoanalyst with a private domain that protects the practitioner from the unrealistic demands of his patients."[39]

In his *Papers on Technique*, Freud admits that there were frequent refusals from patients to use the couch.[40] Since then there have been a number of psychoanalysts who have put forth cases and elaborated on the meaning attached to this.[41] Vision, or lack of vision, seemed to play a predominant role in many of the reported cases, given that most patients feel the need to be able to see the analyst during sessions.[42] But there have also been extensive objections due to the sexual connotations the couch may have for some patients, who may feel vulnerable, exposed, and on display when reclined on the couch. In "A Phobia of The Couch: A Clinical Study of Psychoanalytic

Process", Nancy Kulish discusses various analysts who have written about their patient's refusal to use the couch, and goes into extensive detail regarding her own experience in treating "Ms. S", who refused to use the couch during the first three years of treatment.[43]

Without getting into the details of these cases, it seems fair to say that, refusal or acceptance of the couch, there seems to be an overwhelming ambivalence with regards to this iconic object. The couch appears to play a central role in the uncanny setting of the analyst's office; simultaneously soothing and irritating, comforting and threatening, orienting and disorienting the patient. This oscillating movement anticipates the state of "oceanic" fusion with the object itself; thus, the patient becomes the couch and the couch becomes the patient. This goes beyond pure symbolism of what the couch might represent (the analyst, the mother). Instead, the couch becomes anything that the patient wants to project onto it while in regression; it is an object of possibility. For Winnicott,

> *In so far as the patient is regressed (for a moment or for an hour or over a long period of time) the couch is the analyst, the pillows are breasts, the analyst is the mother at a certain past era. In the extreme it is no longer true to say the couch stands for the analyst.*[44]

II.III Objects within the space

As can be seen from the extensive photographs taken of Freud's Berggasse 19 office in Vienna (see illustration, p 17), he had a vast collection of antique sculpture and imagery from ancient Greece, Rome, Egypt, and the Orient, which he displayed on every available surface.[45] Primitive work is supposed to encourage memory and regression, which might be a reason why Freud engulfed his patients with it. The significance of the collection in his work is also evident in Freud's use of archaeology as a metaphor for psychoanalysis. Nonetheless some critics suggest that the presence of these artifacts is less for the interest of the patient and is more about Freud's own exteriorization of his psyche.[46] Indeed, these interiors are so placated with relics that they seem to be a space of refuge for the collector, where in some instances the patients themselves become part of the collection.[47]

In a detailed analysis of Freud's consultation room in Vienna, Diana Fuss points out how patients would have their first consultation with Freud in his study.[48] They would be seated at a small table adjacent to his writing desk, which was full of collected objects, particularly primitive heads and busts. Across from the table there was a small mirror placed in the plane of the window that would reflect the image of the patient as if to make a bust of the patient which would temporarily join the multitude of his collection.[49]

The London office, where Freud spent his last year, was arranged much like his consultation room at Berggasse 19, yet it did not have a separate study. The consulting room and the study were combined together, with the couch situated opposite his desk. In this space, a large collection of primitive heads was placed adjacent to the end of the couch, where the head of the reclined patient would be during analysis. Curiously, the reclined patient would not see the heads. Freud would see the head of his patient almost align with his collection; a somewhat similar effect caused by the mirror he had in his Viennese study. To a certain extent, Freud's consulting rooms constitute the interiorized scene of his analytical technique; the scene of a relation between subjects mediated by objects. From exploring the role the analyst's office plays in the unfolding of analysis, the space and the objects it contains are of a paradoxical nature capable of producing oscillating, opposing feelings of comfort and alienation; it is a space of the uncanny. This spatial uncanniness pushes the patient into an intermediate state between self and other, becoming in effect a Winnicottian membrane; where things from inside and outside pass through allowing for the emergence of regression.

However, it is important to stress that this uncanniness is not a fixed symbolic quality of the space or the objects within it, rather, as elaborated by Winnicott, it is a fluctuating, dynamic process. For Winnicott, what is important is not the symbology of external objects but their actuality, their condition of possibility. Thus, we are rejecting the view that would reduce external objects, spaces, or buildings to Kleinian symbolizations of good or bad breasts, and advocating for a Winnicottian view of space as possibility, where what is activated during regression is the actual not the symbolic.[50]

Thus, the space of analysis is not just a passive context for treatment; it is an active participant in the analysis. The room activates daydreaming while protecting and sheltering the daydreamer, functioning as a safe haven and shelter for the patient but also as a stimulant of regression. This stimulation is necessarily achieved by enveloping the patient in an environment imbued with qualities of the uncanny. Psychoanalysis and architecture come together through the concept of the uncanny, as explored in the context of the analyst's setting. Interestingly, both are cultural discourses that in themselves embody uncanny qualities, as they deal with what can simultaneously be visible and invisible, comforting and alienating, orienting and disorienting. But fundamentally, both disciplines are activated through the mediation of physical and existential space.

Endnotes

1 Concept of the uncanny as extracted from Freud's "The Uncanny" in *The Standard Edition of the Complete Psychological Works of Sigmund Freud*, vol XVII (1919): *An Infantile Neurosis and Other Works*, London: The Hogarth Press: The Institute of Psycho-Analysis, pp 217–256.

2 Freud first refers to this "oceanic feeling" in *Civilization and its Discontents*, mentioning letters exchanged with his friend now known to be Romain Rolland, letter of December 5, 1927.

3 Freud, *Civilization and its Discontents*. Translated by James Strachey. New York: W.W. Norton & Company, Inc, 1961, p 11.

4 Ibid, p 12.

5 Ibid, pp 69–70.

6 Donald Winnicott, "Mind and its Relation to the Psyche-Soma" in *Through Pediatrics to Psycho-Analysis*, New York: Basic Books, 1975, p 243.

7 According to Winnicott, it is the integration of two types of mothers ("the environmental" and "the instinct" mother) that permits what he calls the distinction between fact and fantasy.

8 Or: what instigates the primary ego to emerge in maturity? What enables the illusion of oneness?

9 Taken from Salman Rushdie's text in memory of Herbert Read (1990), as quoted by Finnish architect Juhani Pallasmaa in a lecture.

10 Gilbert Rose, *The Power of Form. A Psychoanalytic Approach to Aesthetic Form*, Madison, CT: International Press Inc, 1992, p 13.

11 There is potential for relating the Kleinian concept of projective identification with this oceanic state; both entail a melting of boundaries between self and other.

12 Winnicott, "Transitional Objects and Transitional Phenomena" in *Through Pediatrics to Psycho-Analysis,* p 230.

13 Gilbert Rose, *The Power of Form. A Psychoanalytic Approach to Aesthetic Form*, Madison, CT: International Press Inc, 1992, p 92.

14 Ibid, p 195.

15 Ibid, p 235.

16 Adrian Stokes was in analysis with Melanie Klein from 1930 to 1937, and although his writings of this period do not make specific reference to his analysis with her, he was deeply influenced by Kleinian theory.

17 Winnicott, "Metapsychological and Clinical Aspects of Regression within the Psycho-Analytical Set-Up" in *Through Pediatrics to Psycho-Analysis: Collected Papers*, p 286.

18 AC current is produced through a constant change in amplitude and polarity of the electric charge.

19 The English term is not an exact equivalent of the German one; "unheimlich" is translated here throughout by the English "uncanny", but translates literally as unhomely. According to the Oxford English Dictionary, there is a similar ambiguity attached to the English "canny", which may mean not only "cosy" but also "endowed with occult or magical powers".

20 Freud, "The Uncanny", p 219.

21 Ibid, pp 224–225.

22 Anthony Vidler is Dean and Professor at Cooper Union School of Architecture in New York.

23 Anthony Vidler, "Preface" in *The Architectural Uncanny: Essays in the Modern Unhomely,* Cambridge, MA: MIT Press, 1992, pp ix–xiii.

24 Here, we are adopting Stokes's reference to carving and modeling; using it in the context of architectural space evokes the intermediary and multivalent spaces that arise between the modes of carving and modeling.

25 Winnicott, "Metapsychological and Clinical Aspects of Regression", p 278.

26 Ibid, p 285.

27 We are referring to the five senses (sight, hearing, touch, smell, and taste) as conventional although many more primal human senses are believed to exist.

28 The absence of reference to smell in Winnicott's passage allows us to assume that he shares Freud's position on the matter and therefore the sense of smell of a repressed patient would be impaired during treatment, and only full recovery would cure the olfactory canal.

29 Freud, "Letter 66, Extracts from the Fliess Papers" in *The Standard Edition of The Complete Psychological Works of Sigmund Freud*, vol I (1897): *Pre-Psycho-Analytic Publications and Unpublished Drafts*, London: The Hogarth Press: The Institute of Psycho-Analysis, p 269.

30 Here, an indirect reference is being made to the threshold between analyst (chair) and patient (couch).

31 Quote attributed to the architect Juhani Pallasmaa, source unknown.

32 Freud, "On Beginning the Treatment (Further Recommendations on the Technique of Psycho-Analysis I)" in *The Standard Edition of the Complete Psychological Works of Sigmund Freud*, vol XII (1913): *The Case of Schreber, Papers on Technique and Other Works*, London: The Hogarth Press and the Institute of Psycho-analysis, p 134.

33 René Spitz, "Transference: The Analytical Setting and its Prototype" in *International Journal of Psycho-Analysis*, 37 (1956), p 382.

34 Gaston Bachelard, *The Poetics of Space*, Boston: Beacon Press, p 184.

35 Juliet MacCannell, "FreudSpace: Architecture in Psychoanalysis" in *The Annual of Psychoanalysis*, vol 33 (2005), pp 93–107.

36 Jacques Lacan, *The Four Fundamental Concepts of Psycho-Analysis*, Jacques Alain-Miller ed. Translated by Alan Sheridan. New York: Norton, 1998, p 85.

37 MacCannell, "FreudSpace", p 98.

38 George Moraitis describes James Grotstein's affirmation of Freud having discovered the right brain. Moraitis, "Prologue" in *Psychoanalytic Inquiry*, vol 11 (1991), p 257.

39 Moraitis, "The Couch as a Protective Shield for the Analyst" in *Psychoanalytic Inquiry*, vol 15 (1995), p 412.

40 James Strachey (1958). The Standard Edition of the Complete Psychological Works of Sigmund Freud, Volume XII (1911-1913): The Case of Schreber, Papers on Technique and Other Works, ii-vii. The Hogarth Press: The Institute of Psycho-Analysis, London.

41 To name a few: Fenichel, 1941; Glover, 1955; Goldberger, 1995; Greenacre, 1959; Greenson, 1967; Hogan, 1990; Rothstein, 1990; Stone, 1961; Orens 1965; Weissman in 1977; Bergel, 1984; Frank, 1992.

42 As admitted by Freud: "A particularly large number of patients object to being asked to lie down, while the doctor sits out of sight behind them. They ask to be allowed to go through the treatment in some other position, for the most part because they are anxious not to be deprived of a view of the doctor." "On Beginning the Treatment", p 374.

43 Nancy Kulish, "A Phobia of The Couch: A Clinical Study of Psychoanalytic Process" in *Psychoanalytic Quarterly*, 65 (1996), pp 465–494.

44 Winnicott, "Metapsychological and Clinical Aspects of Regression", p 288.

45 Asked by August Aichorn to secretly photograph Freud's living and working environment, the young photographer Edmund Engelman, at great personal risk, took a set of historic photographs of Freud's quarters just before Freud and his family left Vienna after the Nazi occupation of Austria.

46 Charles Rice describing Diana Fuss's interpretation of Freud's antique collection, in *The Emergence of the Interior: Architecture, Modernity, Domesticity*, New York: Routledge, 2007, p 48.

47 Ibid, p 42.

48 Detailed description of Freud's consulting room in Vienna can be found in "Freud's Ear: Berggasse 19" by Diana Fuss (a psychoanalytic critic) and Joel Sanders (an architect), in Fuss, *The Sense of an Interior: Four Writers and the Rooms That Shaped Them*, New York: Routledge, 2004, pp 71–106.

49 Ibid, p 82.

50 To employ symbolism, there has to be a clear distinction between fantasy and fact, inner and outer—something which is absent during the state of fusion, where this separation does not exist.

Bibliography

Bachelard, Gaston. *The Poetics of Space*. Boston: Beacon Press, 1969.

Danze, Elizabeth. "An Architect's View of Introspective Space. The Analytic Vessel" in *The Annual of Psychoanalysis*, 33 (2005), pp 109–124.

Deleuze, Gilles and Claire Parnet. *Dialogues II*. New York: Columbia University Press, 2007.

Forrest, David V. "Elements of Dynamics III: The Face and the Couch" in *Journal of American Academy of Psychoanalysis*, vol 32 (2004), pp 551–564.

Freud, Sigmund. *Civilization and its Discontents*. Translated by James Strachey. New York: W.W. Norton & Company, Inc, 1961.

Freud, Sigmund. "Letter 66, Extracts from the Fliess Papers" in *The Standard Edition of The Complete Psychological Works of Sigmund Freud*, vol I (1897): *Pre-Psycho-Analytic Publications and Unpublished Drafts*, Psychoanalytic Electronic Publishing, pp 268–271.

Freud, Sigmund. "On Beginning the Treatment (Further Recommendations on the Technique of Psycho-Analysis I)" in *The Standard Edition of the Complete Psychological Works of Sigmund Freud*, vol XII (1913): *The Case of Schreber, Papers on*

Technique and Other Works. London: The Hogarth Press: The Institute of Psycho-Analysis, pp 121–144.

Freud, Sigmund. "Project for a Scientific Psychology" in *The Standard Edition of the Complete Psychological Works of Sigmund Freud*, vol I (1886): *Pre-Psycho-Analytic Publications and Unpublished Drafts*, pp 281–391.

Freud, Sigmund. "The Uncanny" in *The Standard Edition of the Complete Psychological Works of Sigmund Freud*, vol XVII (1919): *An Infantile Neurosis and Other Works*, pp 217–256.

Fuss, Diana. *The Sense of An Interior: Four Writers and The Rooms That Shaped Them*. New York: Routledge, 2004.

Grotstein, J.S. "Inner Space: Its Dimensions and its Coordinates" in *International Journal of Psycho-Analysis*, 59 (1978), pp 55–61.

Kulish, Nancy. "A Phobia of The Couch: A Clinical Study of Psychoanalytic Process" in *Psychoanalytic Quarterly*, 65 (1996), pp 465–494.

Lacan, Jacques. "The Direction of the Treatment and the Principles of its Power" in *Écrit: A Selection*. New York: Norton, 1977, pp 250–310.

Lacan, Jacques. *The Four Fundamental Concepts of Psycho-Analysis*. Edited by Jacques Alain-Miller and translated by Alan Sheridan. New York: Norton, 1998.

Lambert, Gregg. "Deterritorializing Psycho-analysis" in *Derrida, Deleuze, Psychoanalysis*. Edited by Gabriele Schwab. New York: Columbia University Press, 2007, pp 192–211–XX.

Loewald, Hans W. "Hypnoid State, Repression, Abreaction and Recollection" in *Journal of the American Psychoanalytic Association*, 3 (1955), pp 201–210.

MacCannell, Juliet. "FreudSpace: Architecture in Psychoanalysis" in *The Annual of Psychoanalysis*, vol 33 (2005), pp 93–107.

Moraitis, George. "Prologue" in *Psychoanalytic Inquiry*, vol 11 (1991), pp 257–260.

Moraitis, George. "The Couch as a Protective Shield for the Analyst" in *Psychoanalytic Inquiry*, vol 15 (1995), pp 406–412.

Merleau-Ponty, Maurice. *The Primacy of Perception*. Edited by James M. Edie. Chicago: Northwestern University Press, 1964.

Pallasmaa, Juhani. *The Eyes of the Skin: Architecture and the Senses*. Chichester, UK: John Wiley, 2005.

Parr, Adrian. "Deterritorialization/ Reterritorialization" in *The Deleuze Dictionary*. Edited by Adrian Parr. New York: Columbia University Press, 2005, pp 66–69.

Rice, Charles. *The Emergence of The Interior: Architecture, Modernity, Domesticity*. New York: Routledge, 2007.

Rose, Gilbert. *The Power of Form. A Psychoanalytic Approach to Aesthetic Form*. Madison, CT: International Press Inc, 1992.

Silverman, Kaja. *The Threshold of The Visible World*. New York: Routledge, 1996.

Spitz, René. "Transference: The Analytical Setting and its Prototype" in *International Journal of Psycho-Analysis*, 37 (1956), pp 380–385.

Stokes, Adrian. "Form in Art" in *New Directions in Psycho-Analysis*. Edited by Melanie Klein, Paula Heimann, R. Money-Kyrle. London: Routledge, 2003.

Stokes, Adrian. "Psycho-Analysis and our Culture" in *Contemporary Psychoanalysis*, 10 (1974), pp 469–482.

Vidler, Anthony. *The Architectural Uncanny: Essays in the Modern Unhomely*. Cambridge, MA: MIT Press, 1992.

Winnicott, Donald W. "Metapsychological and Clinical Aspects of Regression within the Psycho-Analytical Set-Up", "Mind and its Relation to the Psyche-Soma" and "Transitional Object and Transitional Phenomena" in *Through Pediatrics to Psycho-Analysis: Collected Papers*. New York: Basic Books, 1975, pp 278–294, pp 243–254, and pp 229–242.

Illustrations

***The Ambassadors* by Hans Holbein**, p 54. Frontal and anamorphic view, www.designboom.com/history/mirror/25.jpg laloli.files.wordpress.com/2008/08/holbein_ambassadors_anamorphosis.jpg.

We were invited to participate in the first annual Flatiron Plaza competition in 2014. The brief called for something festive that would engage visitors during the holidays and serve to reactivate the plaza, which was situated across from the famous Flatiron building in New York. This was an emblematic space yet not as vibrant as local community members wanted it to be.

Our proposal brings together public engagement and movement through a nebulous formation of "social spheres" that join, merge, and fuse to create a landscape of social possibilities where people gather and engage in various activities while also having their perception of the site reframed. For this project, we had to strive for what might seem paradoxical; physical interactivity that allows playful interaction from visitors and passersby while ensuring the sturdiness needed for a public project that must withstand New York crowds and winter weather.

The skin of the structure is created by a dense network of loosely hanging strips that move to make visible the movement of wind and people. At night, the interiors are lit with colored light, creating glowing effects with this shimmering skin. The color scheme mirrors effects that are already present in New York City landmarks, and symbolically celebrates the diversity of winter festivities by different groups—Jewish, European, African American, and Native American would each have a color representing their celebration. The physical interactivity affords a playful relationship between visitor and installation, while the compact mode of assembly, harnessing digital design and physical fabrication, ensures the installation is sturdy enough to withstand the crowds and the weather.

Our aim was to recognize the emblematic nature of the Flatiron site while also allowing an uncanny reframing of perceptions. Each social sphere is positioned strategically in order to reorient the visitor with unique views of the famous building from within and between the different spheres.

floor plan

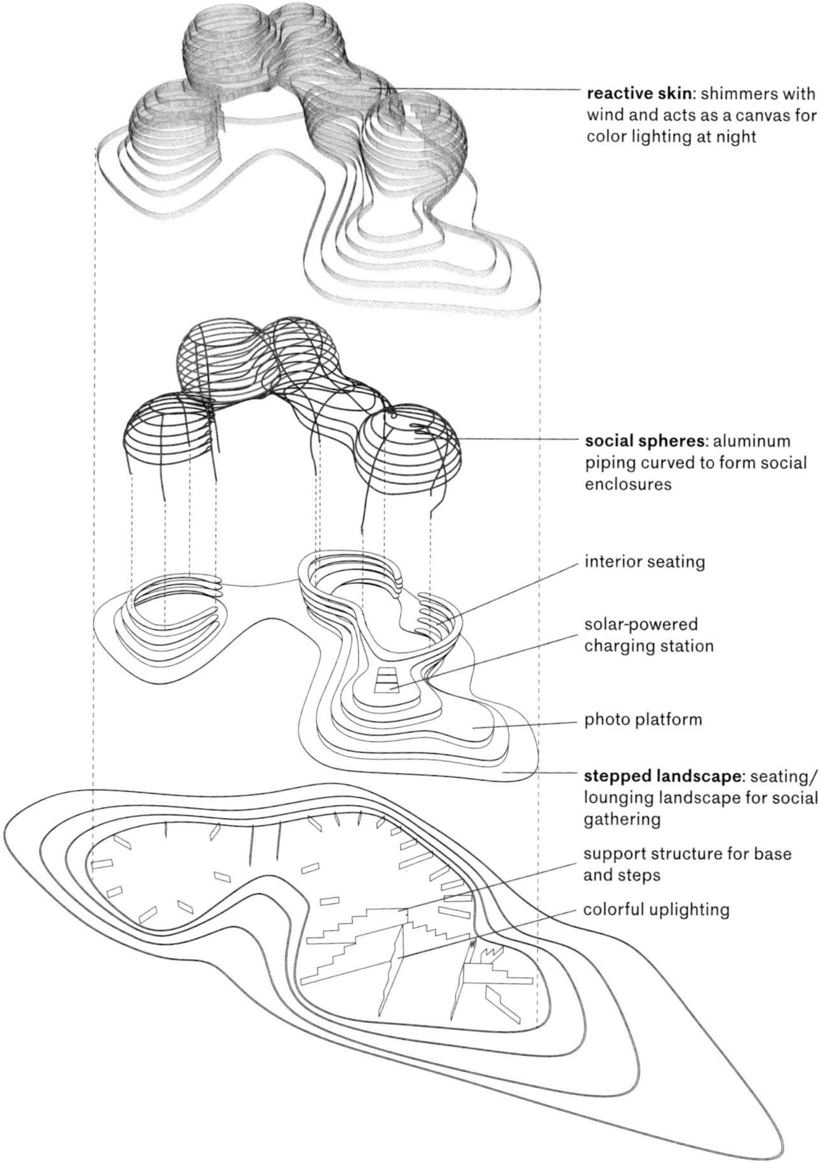

exploded view of installation elements

Project data

- **Location** New York City
- **Design** Eva Perez de Vega + Ian Gordon
- **Organization** Flatiron Partnership and Van Alen Institute

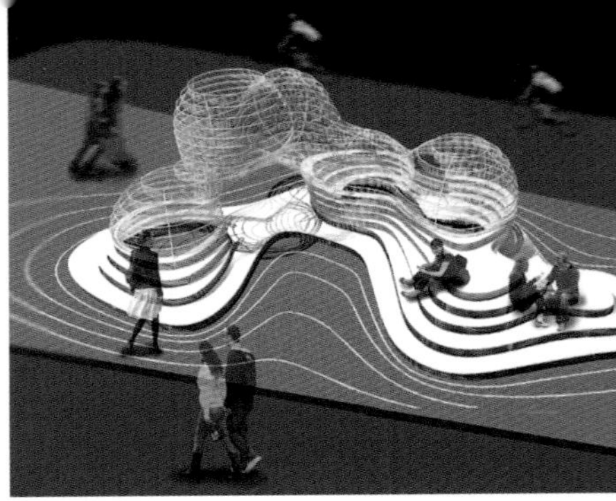

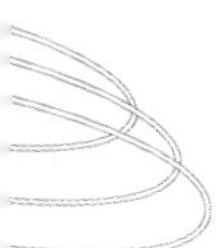

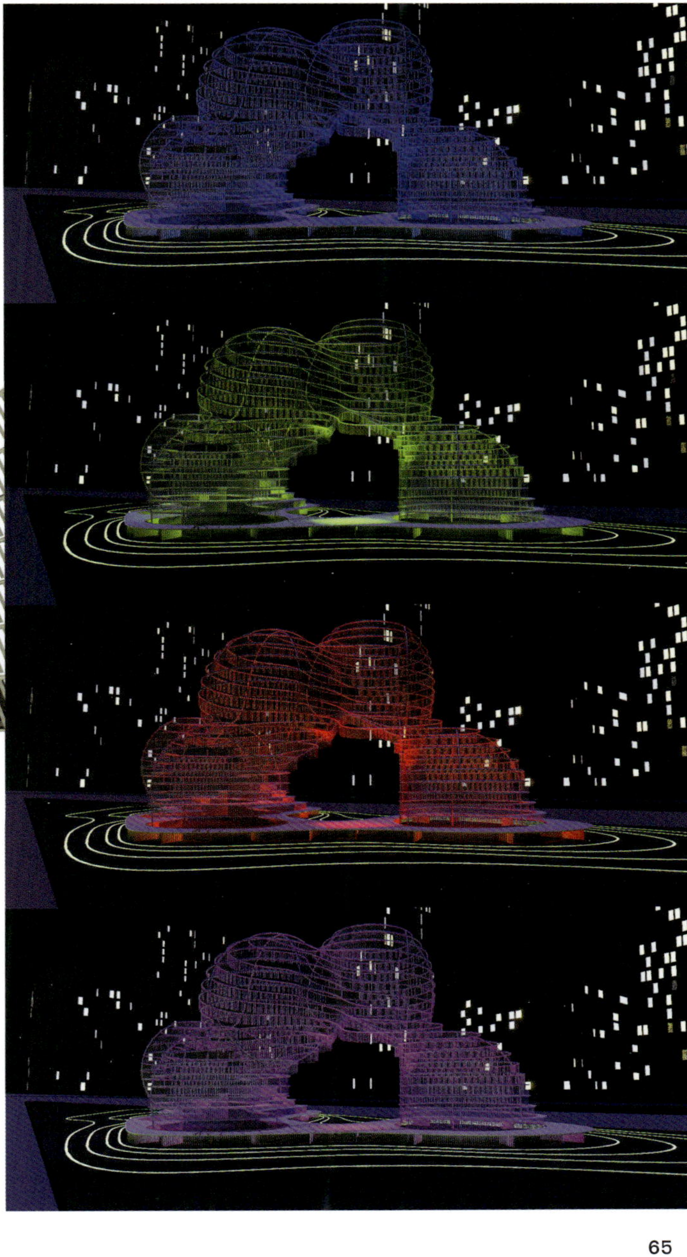

evolve physical therapy

2017

We were approached by a physical therapy team to help them expand their growing practice by creating a new space for their clients on the Upper East Side.

The existing space was a bland commercial space with generic drop-in ceiling tiles and wall partitions that fragmented a convoluted U-shape plan. The space felt cramped, with minimal natural light entering from a multilevel interior atrium along one side of the space. There is often little recognition on how spaces make us "feel", but for a patient entering physical therapy, trying to heal one's bodily trauma, the mental condition, exacerbated by the environment one finds oneself in, is critical.

We approached this project with the goal of unifying the disjointed U-shaped plan visually and spatially, to create a sense of ease and calm for the patient entering into therapy. This was achieved by replacing the bathroom with a new accessible one that could double as a changing room for patients, and by removing all static partitions for a sense of flow and serenity. In addition to opening up the space as much as possible for therapy sessions and physical workouts, the entrance, lobby, waiting room, reception area, and therapy space were visually and physically tied together by the addition of a sculptural ceiling structure made of curved wood that gestures dynamically toward the depth of the U-shaped space. A continuous recessed linear cove lighting element in the ceiling flows along the ceiling gesture to emphasize the sense of dynamic continuity of program and space.

Coincidentally, one of the partners of e+i, Eva, had a bike accident during the construction of this project, which resulted in a badly broken arm and the need for extensive physical therapy after reconstructive surgery. This strengthened the disbelief in the notion of the body as distinct from the mind, and reinforced the ties between emotional state and the making of physical space.

evolve

SCIFIT

Project data

- **Location** New York City
- **Design** Eva Perez de Vega + Ian Gordon
- **Organization** Evolve Physical Therapy
- **Fabrication** NYC Builders

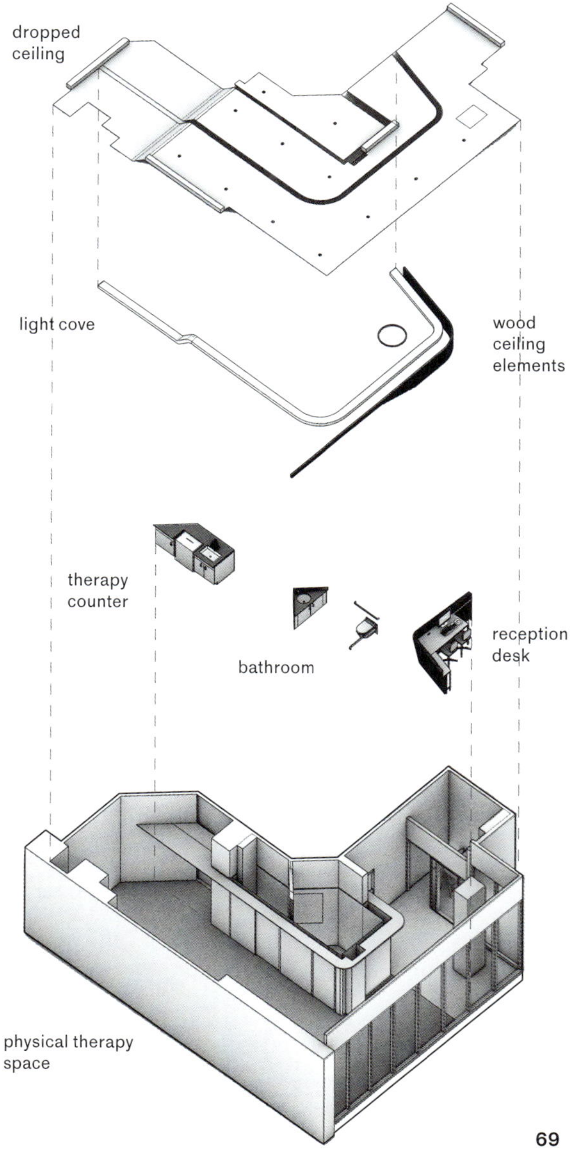
dropped
ceiling
light cove
wood
ceiling
elements
therapy
counter
bathroom
reception
desk
physical therapy
space

parachute pavilion

2005

The irresistible synthetic nature of Coney Island's early days sets the stage for a pavilion of unnatural phenomena that shift us through various pleasures; aesthetic, culinary, cultural, and commercial, where unexpected spaces and programs unfold.

The Parachute Pavilion is thus a journey into new synthetic landscapes, both interior and exterior, that constantly redefine Coney Island's position in history and what it can become in the future. The landscape begins with an undulating roofscape that captures reflections of the sun and sea, and defines the programmed areas below. The continuity of the roof's standing seams is interrupted by parachute-like structures that puncture it and extend below toward the programmed spaces, hovering over them as unnatural glowing objects. These pods are specially programmed spaces that envelop us and serve as eyes that turn their gaze toward the parachute jump landmark, visually reconnecting us to Coney Island.

The building is porous at boardwalk level, allowing direct access to the parachute pods, and flowing circulation through the main spaces, with views into the restaurant and event spaces below. The restaurant space has two areas, which, while remaining continuous, offer visitors a choice of a full-service restaurant or a more casual café with a bar. The former is equipped with seating pods—an integrated system of table, seating, and lighting—that can be rolled into position by the visitor, offering great flexibility and an ever-changing landscape of furniture arrangements. The event space is a large flexible double-height space that can be divided to host different events. The store and offices are located in a glazed curved volume that hovers over the boardwalk entrance.

The synthetic and natural landscapes proposed, envisioned for sites below and above the boardwalk, attempt to reinterpret and thus reinvent the Coney Island beachfront for the twenty-first century.

exploded view of project levels

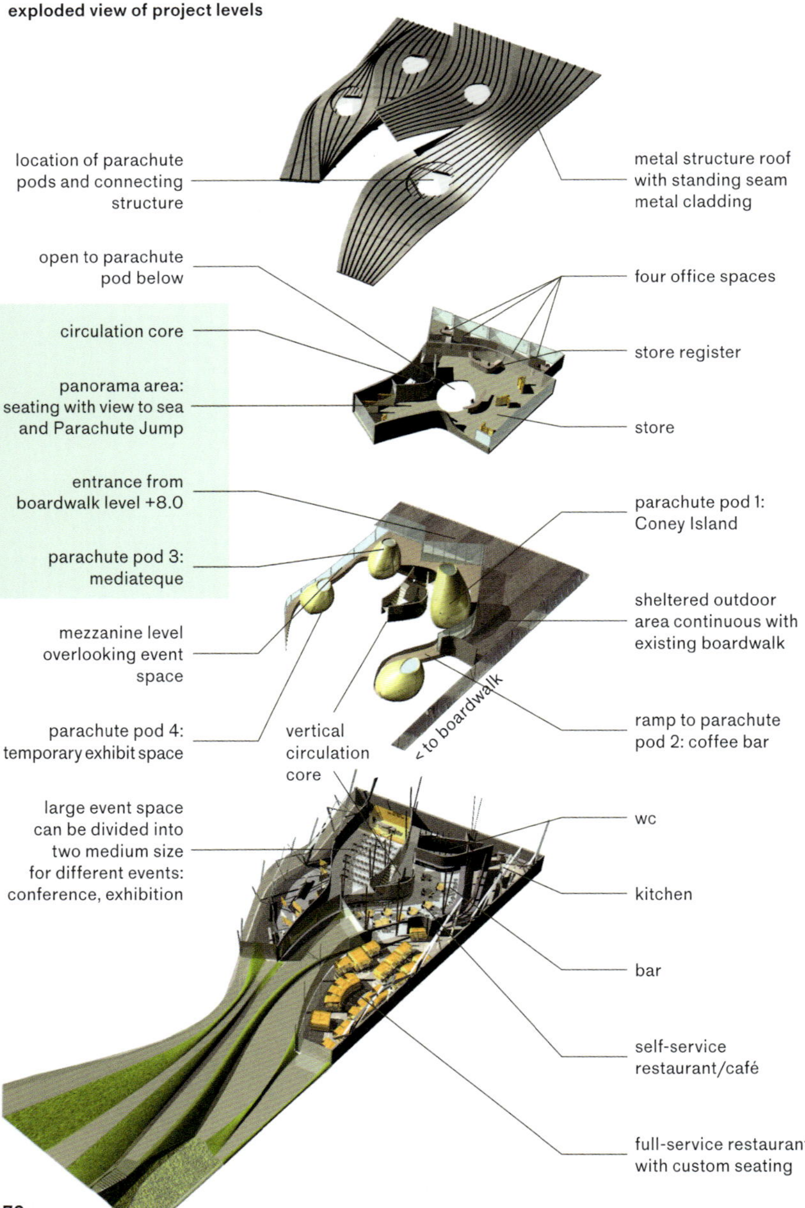

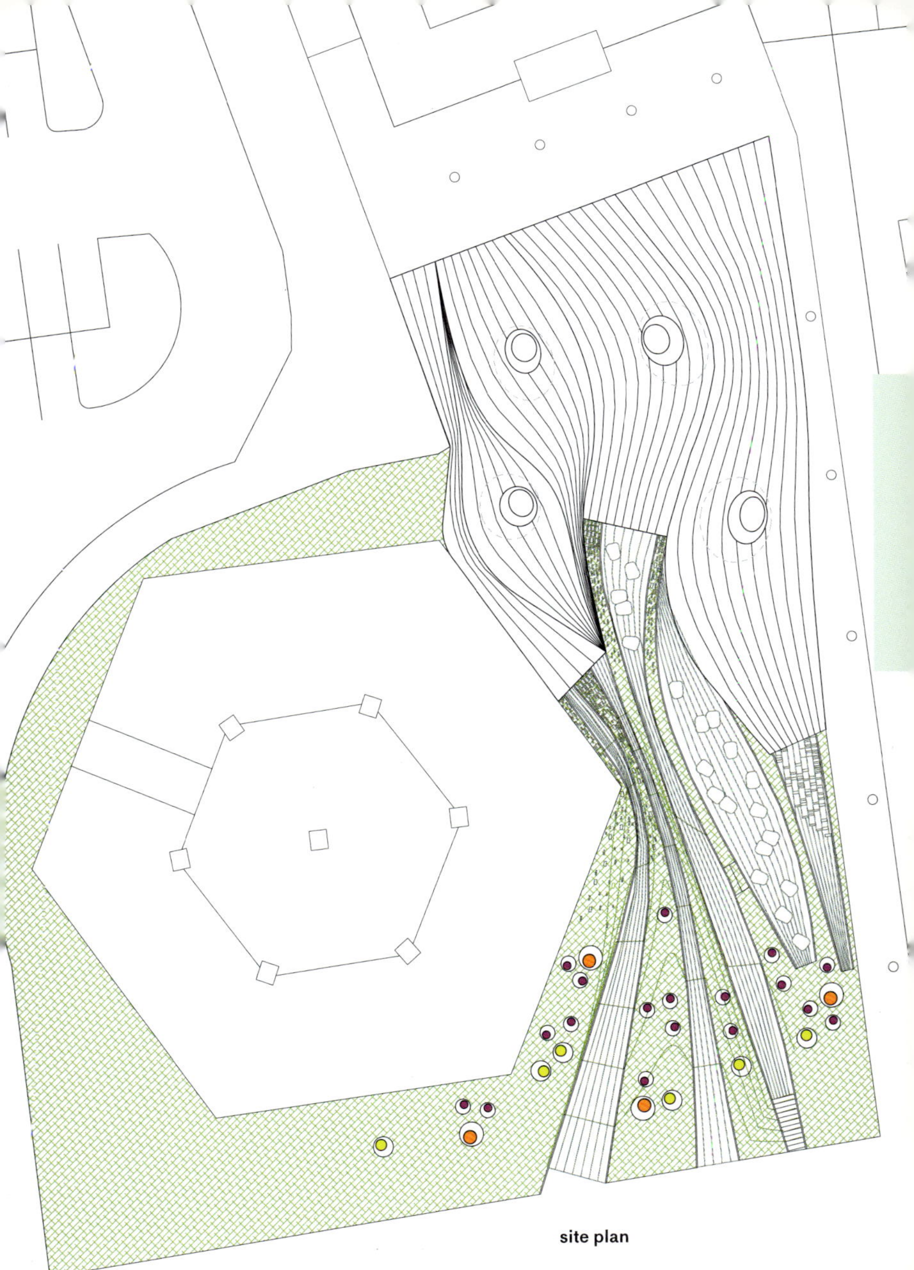

site plan

Project data

- **Location** New York City
- **Design** Eva Perez de Vega
- **Organization** Van Alen Institute
- **Award** Beachscape prize

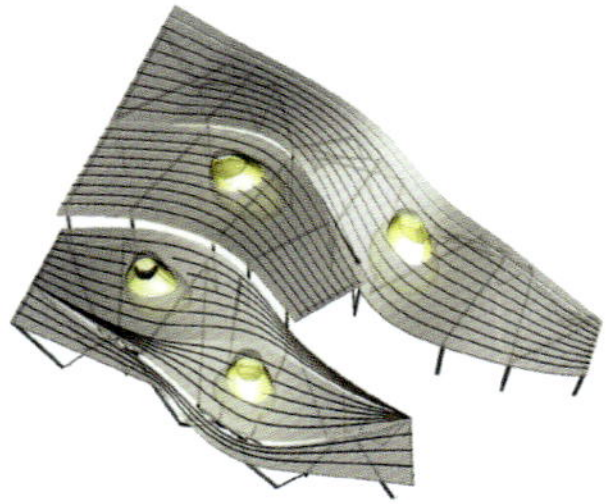

roof structure

second floor

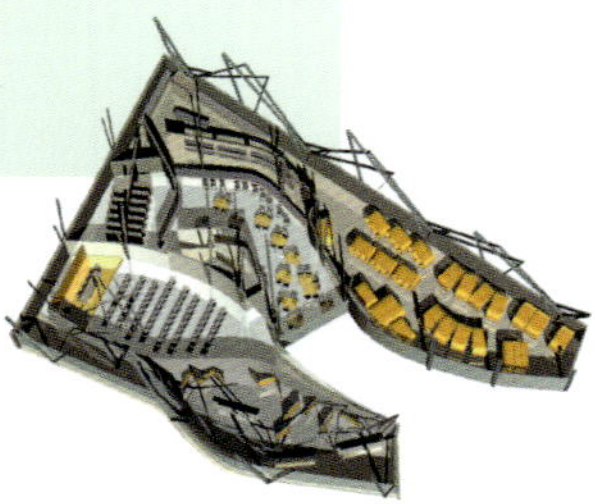

ground floor

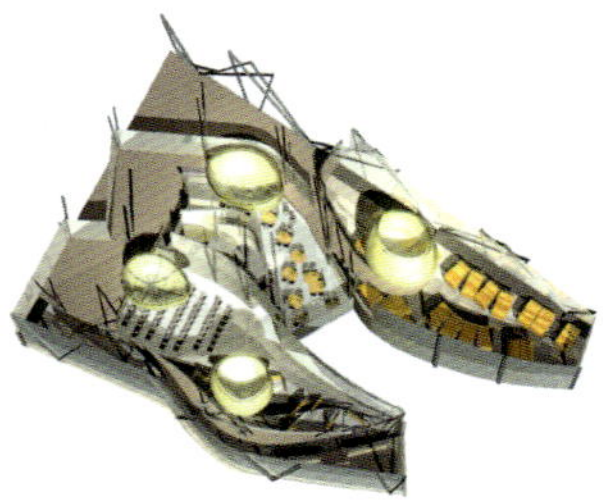

first floor

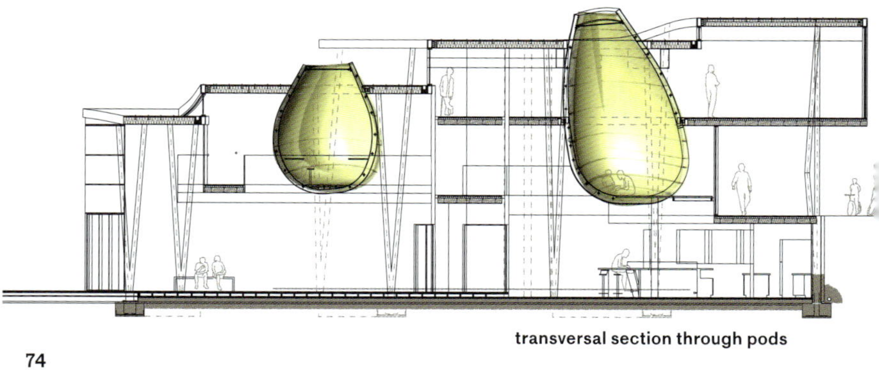

transversal section through pods

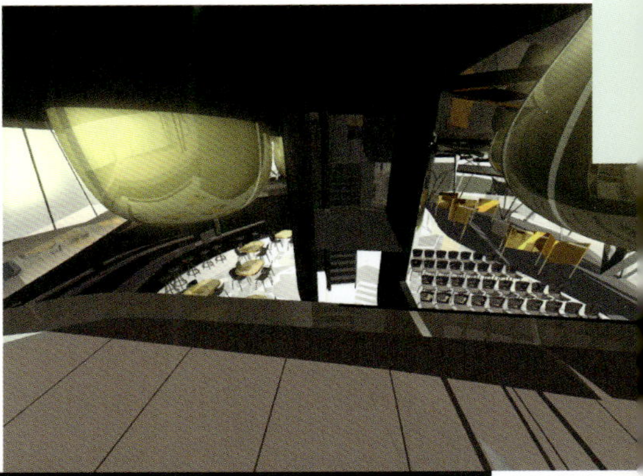

chinatown gateway

2018

New York City's Chinatown is at a pivotal moment in its history. While locals and tourists alike clearly recognize that it is important to uphold Chinatown's traditional values and cultural heritage, there is also a desire to push it toward the future, expanding it beyond what it has been typically recognized for, and to invite everyone to learn about the breadth of what Chinatown has to offer. As members of Chinatown's community (e+i has its office in Chinatown, and the two partners also reside in the area with children who go to local schools), we understand the importance of acknowledging the heritage of the area while also responding to the needs of a changing culture.

Our goal for the project is to create an iconic gesture on the site that entices neighbors and tourists alike to connect and engage with it. Our gateway speaks of movement, passage, and change, while also providing a space for interacting with each other on the piazza-like steps, offering possibilities for the community to gather and come together. For us, a gateway is not about creating an icon that is seen from afar, but rather about connecting with local communities, enabling them to be propelled into the future while also recognizing the heritage of the site.

The Chinatown Gateway is conceived as a portal and passageway between the Chinatown community and adjacent Little Italy and SoHo neighborhoods, as well as the active tourist population. The pavilion creates a new multipurpose public space, which also accommodates larger community gatherings typical in Chinatown.

The project harnesses the unique site conditions into a dramatic form highly attuned to the prow-like location. Stunning effects come into play when the form is viewed from the prow of the site from which the project seems to collapse into a single vertical line. When the pavilion is viewed from Canal Street, the form evokes traditional shapes such as the Chinese pagoda roof and hutong hut that inspired it, while maintaining a contemporary formal gesture.

The oculus is a literal passageway across the site and a virtual connector via interactive technologies, which are networked to have reach far beyond the site's footprint.

The project fuses a contemporary form with nuanced references to traditional Chinese architecture: the tiled roof, wood cladding, and sinuous curves are evocative of eastern motifs while also offering a striking contemporary geometry.

EVENT
CALENDAR
EVENT
CALENDAR

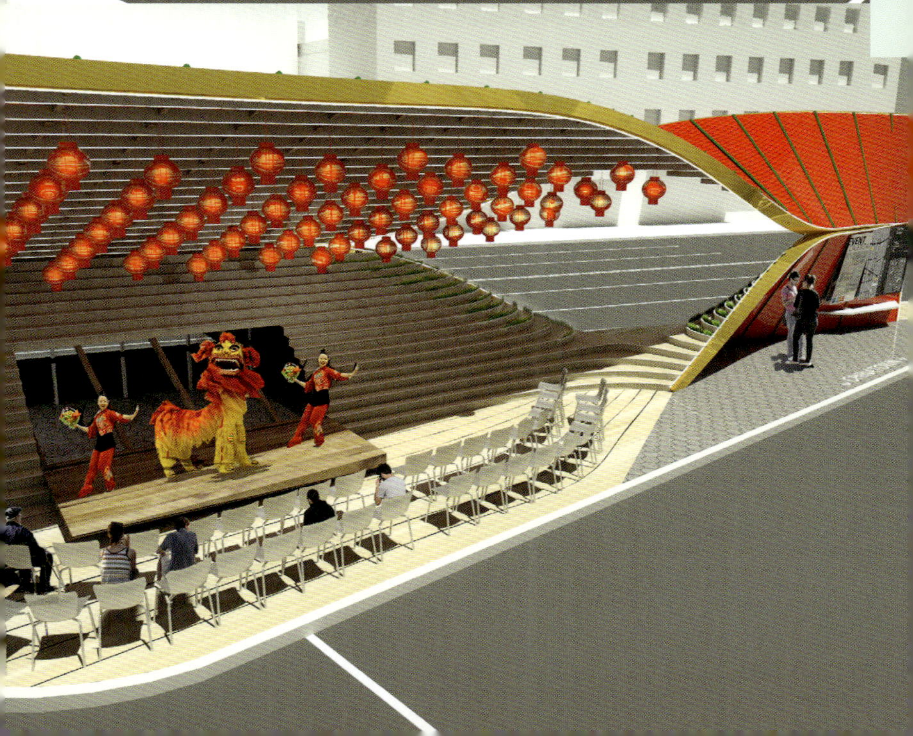

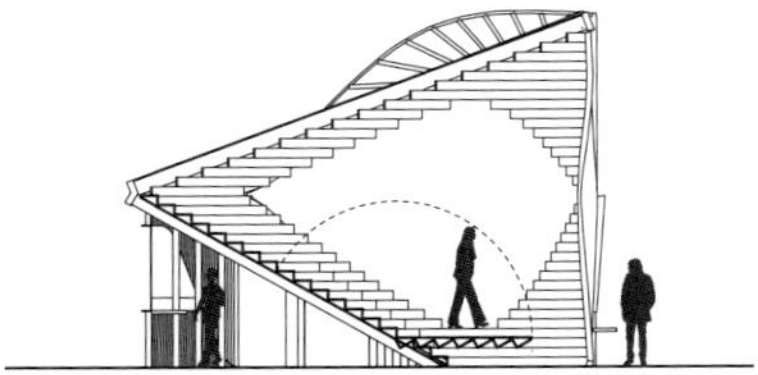

section x1

section x5

section x2

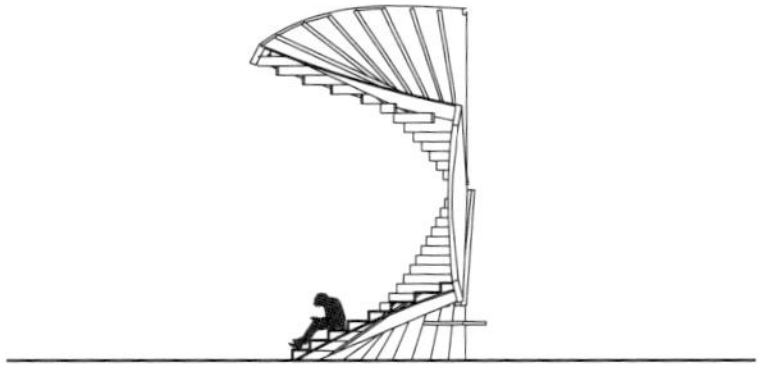

section x6

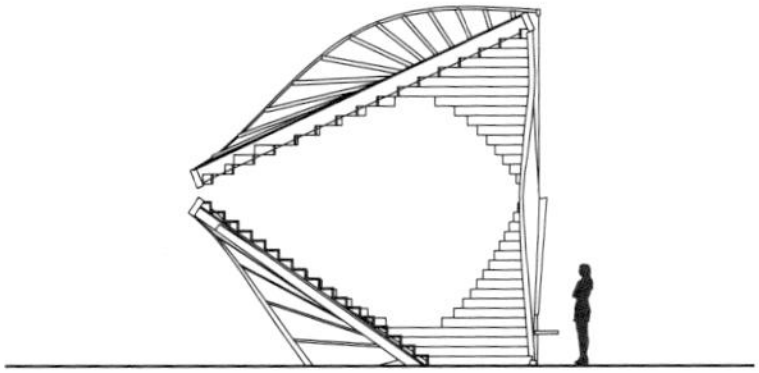

section x3

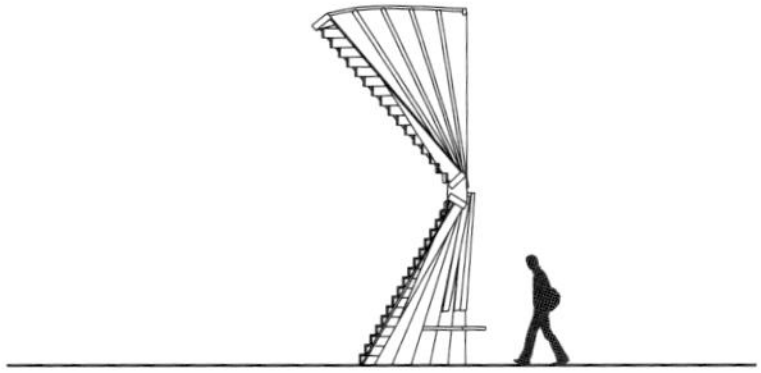

section x7

section x4

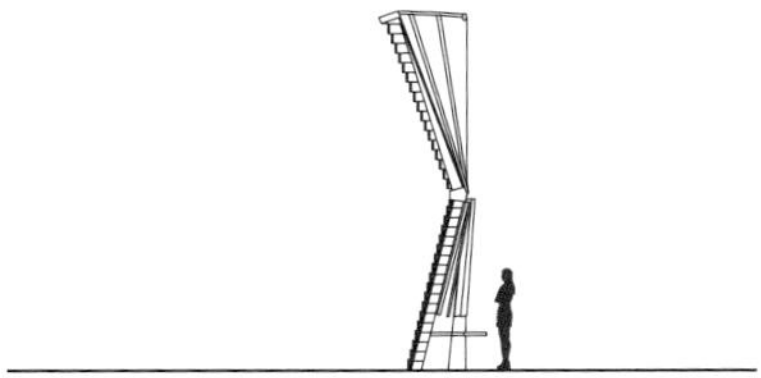

section x8

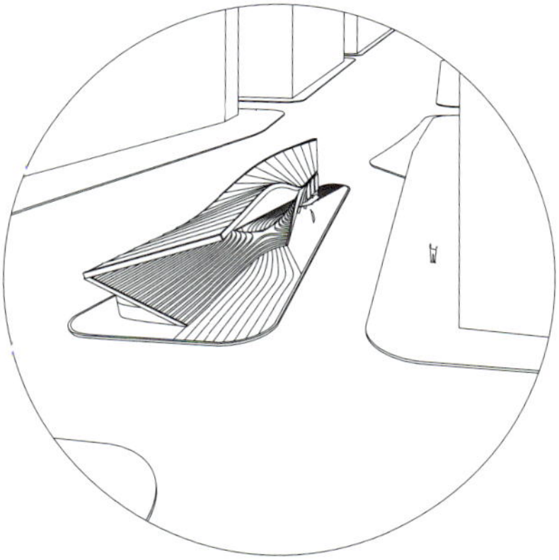

scenario 1

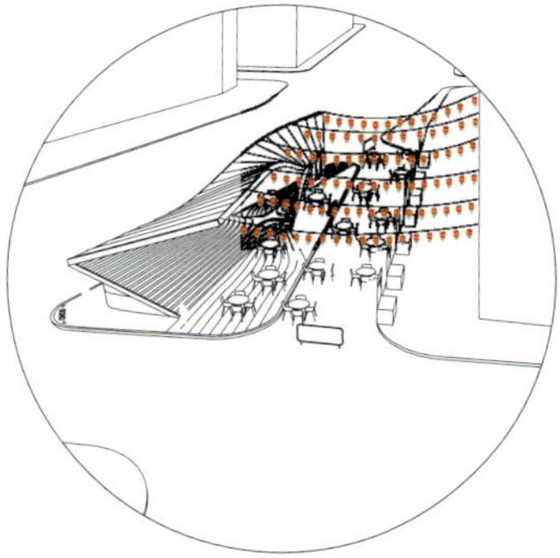

scenario 2

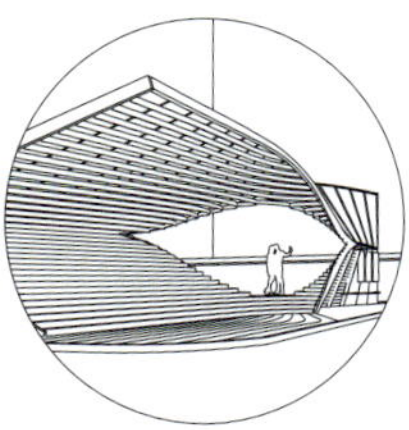

photo moment

photo moment

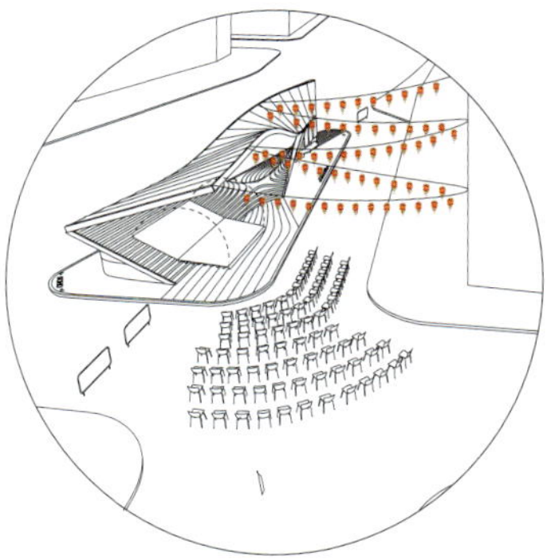

scenario 3

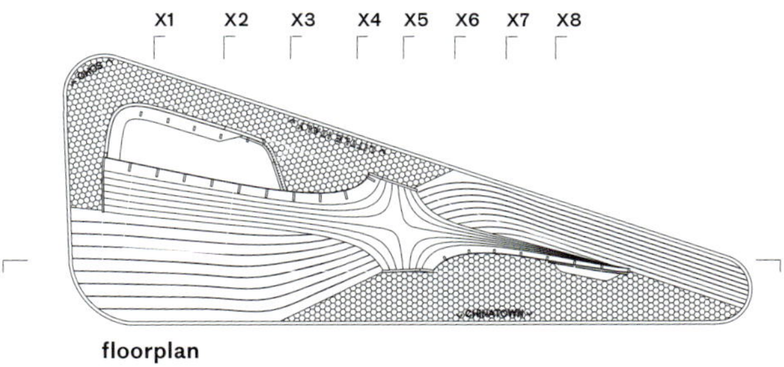

floorplan

Project data

- **Location** New York City
- **Design** Eva Perez de Vega + Ian Gordon
- **Assistant** Sidhant Seth
- **Organization** Department of Transportation
- **Structural Consultant** Zak Kostura, ARUP
- **Lighting Consultant** Jacinda Ross, ARUP
- **Code Consulting** Conversano Associates
- **Chinese Culture Consultant** Yeshu Tan
- **Award** Finalist selection
- **Posthuman render** Erika Hrivikova

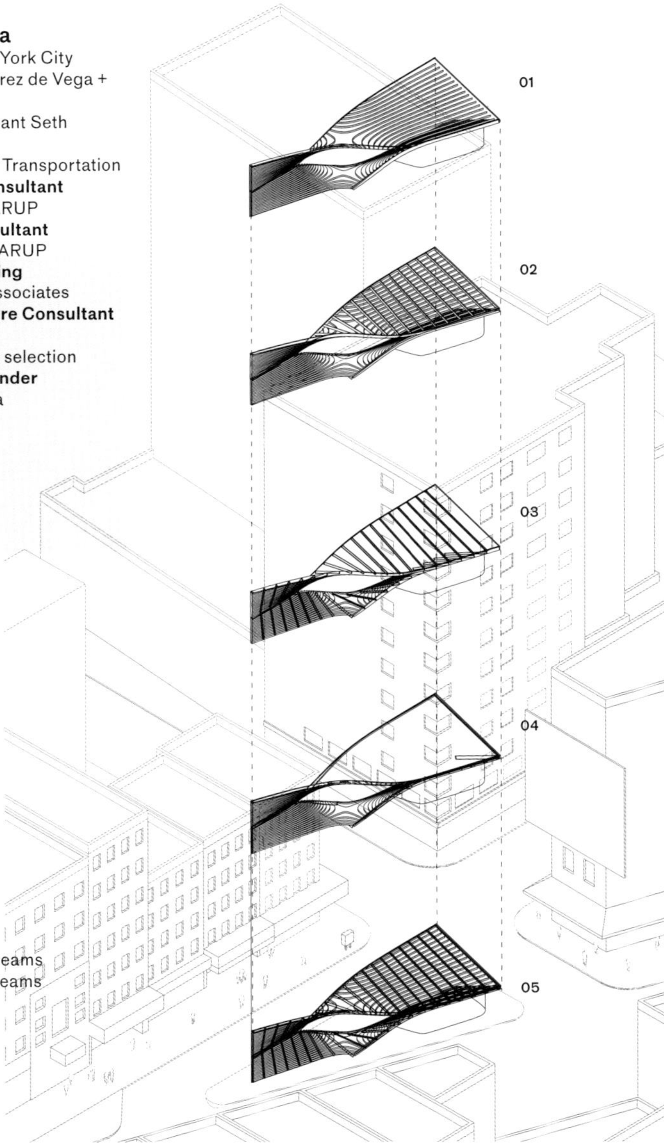

01 ribs
02 framework
03 horizontal beams
04 perimeter beams
05 project

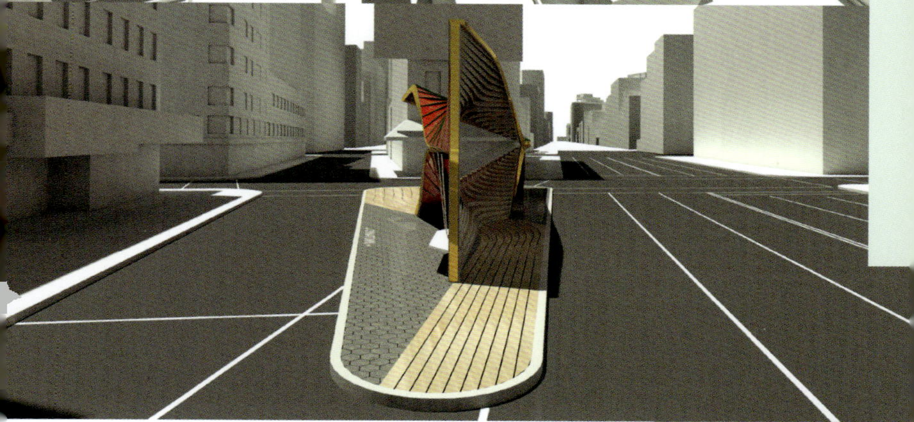

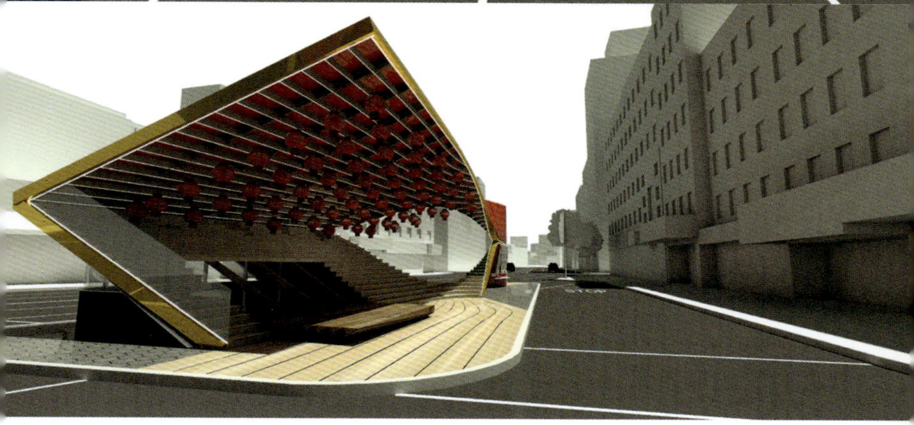

OPPOSITE This project is imagined with species that are now verging on extinction in the region—the eastern cougar and short-eared owl—flourishing the architecture, with the American lotus peppers along Canal Street, which returns to its origins as a shallow canal connecting the eastern and western coasts of Manhattan.

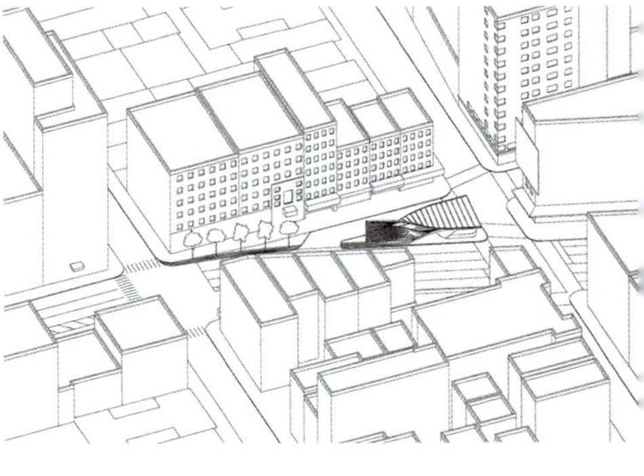

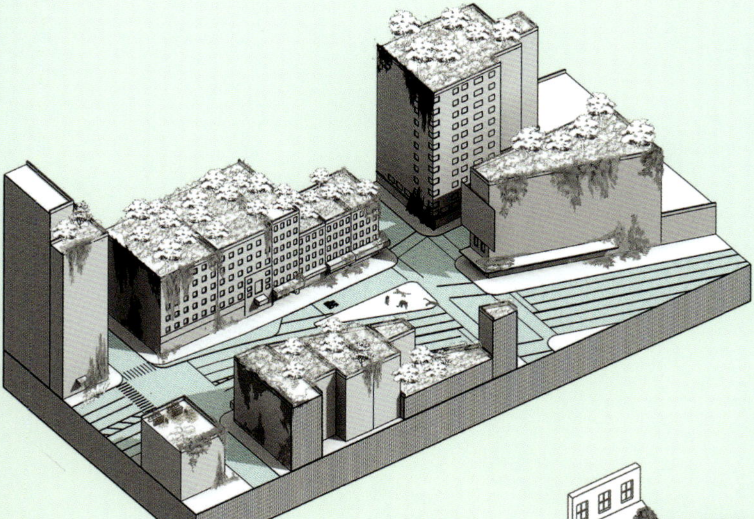

2050 alternative

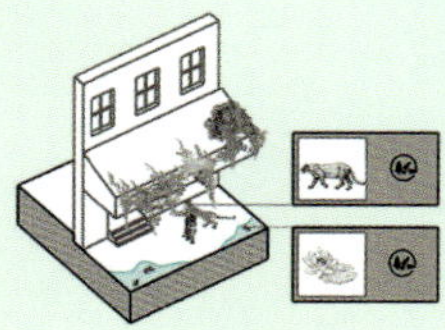

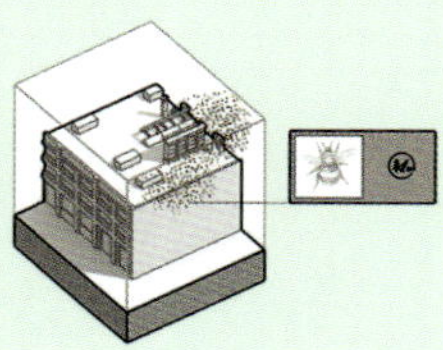

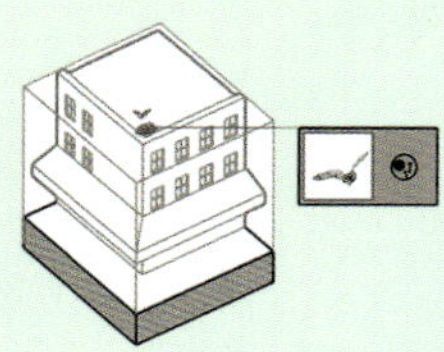

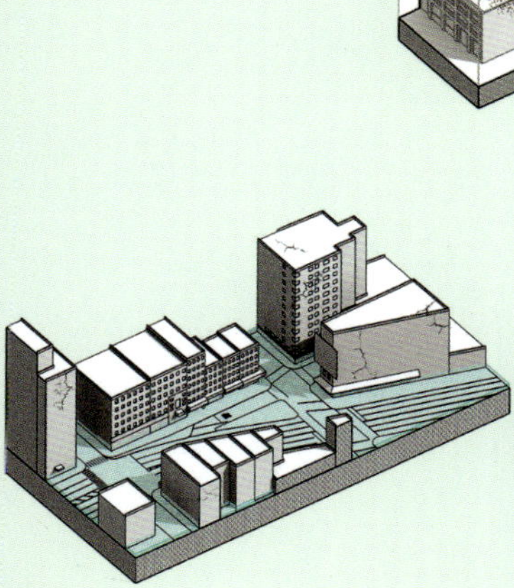

2050

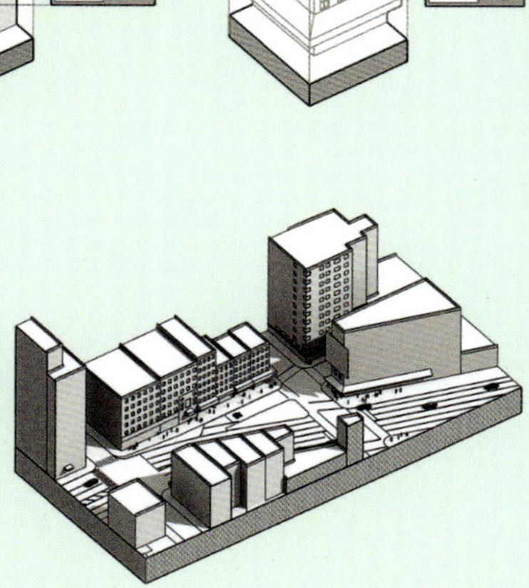

present

piazza
ceramica

daegu public
library

gather

dubrovnik
behind
the city urban
development

highbridge
museum
in the clouds

86

Philosophy of history expressed through architecture

The prevailing attitude sees historical knowledge as being part of the realm of language in the form of texts, discourses, ideologies, and metaphors. Indeed, while history is mostly communicated through generations via written or oral means, the philosophical expression of history—its historicity—also exists in its non-linguistic manifestation, most saliently, through our built environment.

I Historical expressivity

I.I Historical knowledge

Wilhelm Dilthey was particularly interested in the role that history played in our understanding of the present. Beyond the mere recounting or even the interpretation of events, for Dilthey, history has the capacity to liberate us, to set us free, because it "lifts us from the burden of present."[1] History gives us a larger and different perspective on our life so that we can realize that not everything is the way it appears to be for us in the present. For Dilthey, humanity cannot understand itself through reflection or introspection, but through history. He wants to emphasize that man's understanding is dependent on past worldviews, interpretations, and a shared world, so that there is a temporality to historical knowledge.[2] For him, human beings are historical beings, intertwined with the history of past lives and cultures. However, if this is the case, then those who write history are already writing it from a given philosophical point of view, imbued with the biases and philosophy of that particular historical moment: "history can tell him ... never in objective concepts but always only in the living experience which springs up out of the depths of his own being."[3]

Dilthey's ambitious project involves delving into the question of how historical knowledge is even possible. To tackle a possible answer, he makes a distinction between two forms of knowledge: knowledge of natural science and knowledge of humanities. For him, historical knowledge cannot be reduced to empirical knowledge of the past, rather, what makes historical knowledge possible is knowledge of humanities that are linked to certain categories that express humanity. In this text, the interest is in broadening the notion of how this humanity can be expressed, by first exploring Dilthey's categories of historical expressivity, and then proposing another realm that he leaves largely unexplored: that of the built environment—the architecture that has housed humanity.

I.II Manifestations of life

Wilhelm Dilthey is interested in exploring how the understanding of other persons and their manifestations of life can contribute to historical knowledge. Manifestations of life are not deliberate attempts to express something explicitly but rather despite there not being a purposeful intent to communicate or project a specific meaning, it nonetheless makes it understandable. In Dilthey's words, these are manifestations that "without any intent to express spirit nevertheless make it understandable".[4]

Dilthey considers manifestations of life to emerge in a series of "classes": the first of these classes is concepts and thought formations. He holds that such thought formations, being tied to science, can be detached from their particular context and exist independently of the time or the people involved in forming it. He believes that this class of manifestations of life is held by the principle of identity, whereby the judgment is the same for the person who formulates it as for the person who understands it. The second class is actions, which emerge not from a wish to communicate anything in particular, but there is a relationship between an action, what it expresses of the human spirit, and the assumptions these actions allow us to make. In this case, the interpretation of these actions will always be imbued with the preconceptions and baggage of the era in which they are being interpreted. Thus, the state of mind of the people involved in such actions must be known and considered when interpreting the significance of the action itself. Given that we may have deliberated before acting, the action itself cannot tell us that much about the inner life that gave rise to the action, so the deed expresses only part of the being. It is the third class, expressions of lived experience, that gives us more insight into the "psychic life", because it emerges from "depths not illuminated by consciousness". However, these expressions can also be deceptive because they require interpretation which is determined at that moment and is therefore conditioned by that moment. Interestingly, Dilthey gives us a hint as to when this deception of interpretation can be avoided: "But when in a great work a spiritual content is liberated from its creator, whether it be a poet, artist, or writer, we enter a realm where deception ends."[5]

For Dilthey, a great work of art is also a "truthful" work of art that does not want to say anything about its author; it exists independently of the knowing or the doing of the artist. Reliable understanding of such work "arises in the confines between knowing and doing, a sphere in which life discloses itself at a depth inaccessible to observation, reflection, and theory".[6]

Dilthey's concept of manifestations of life, while intended to be applied to language,[7] is quite relevant to architecture, because without wanting to express or communicate something explicitly, it nonetheless does so, and can tell us quite a bit about the beliefs and attitudes of the era in which it was built.

Architecture could also be interpreted as a piece of writing, by trying to explore its meaning, understanding the era in which it was built and parsing the motivations of the authors.[8] However, it can also be simply experienced independently of its meaning and intended messages; it choreographs human movement and, in so doing, restricts or enables certain things to happen.

In other words, it exists independently of the author while still expressing quite a bit of its original intentionality through the experience of it. Architecture need not be read linguistically, despite the wish of many to do so; its spatial and material expression is in itself an objective manifestation of life.

I.III Experience and time: music and architecture

Dilthey mostly emphasizes language as the art where "the life of mind and spirit finds its complete and exhaustive expression" while also being intimately tied to personal contact and interpretation, or what he calls exegesis.[9] Written records of human existence, which are the basis for philology (as the art of writing) and hermeneutics (as its science), are interpreted with hopes of making objective comprehension possible while necessarily connected to criticism and interpretation. Dilthey privileges language as the expression of human experience, but he also gives us a glimpse into the significance of other non-linguistic expression:

> *Every square planted with trees, every room in which chairs are arranged, is understandable to us from childhood because human tendencies to set goals, produce order, and define values in common have assigned a place to every square and every object in the room.*[10]

From Dilthey's thoughts on the significance of built space, he seems to be alluding to the fact that we can gain knowledge of the built environment without being specifically instructed on how to understand it, because it is part of our historicity. It is understandable to us from childhood because every arrangement of furniture in a space or of a plant in a garden is already imbued with the history of it being done before and guided by our tendencies to set goals. Dilthey does give a special place to the arts (in particular, music), claiming that it, too, can be the expression of lived experience. Additionally, expression in the context of music is given a special meaning:

> *[it] designates an imaginative process in which lived experience illuminates the historically evolved world of tones in which all the ways of being expressive have been connected in the historical continuity of the tradition.*[11]

For Dilthey, historical knowledge is built out of our lived experience and we extract a sense of meaning from the temporal flow. Much like in a musical melody, which is experienced in time as an unfolding of the musical notes, history and lived experience are also an unfolding of events in time. In this sense, history is always in the process of becoming, where new events actually have the capacity to shed light on past events. Many have made an analogy between history and a story, a narrative, where we can only understand the meaning of the story when we arrive at the end of it. Dilthey also makes an analogy of the parts–whole relationship with musical notes and a melody; it is not until the notes come together that the music becomes intelligible. For Dilthey, music has the capacity to give expression to human experience.

Similarly, architecture is the material manifestation of human experience. Much like music, it is experienced in time, even though its temporality is different; we can no longer hold onto the linearity of the unfolding of the original time of a historical event. When we experience the built environment, which may be an expression of a particular historical moment, there is a new temporality, which responds to a present condition but is somehow tainted with the past, in a way that it obliges us to look forward to the future. History, music, and architecture all require us to hold onto what has passed but also to project something into the future. There is an imaginative dimension to the expression of history. Indeed, architecture can be seen as a material expression of our humanity.

II Architectural historicity

> *The historical world is always there, and the individual does not merely contemplate it from without but is intertwined with it.*[12]

Unlike Descartes, Dilthey believes that historical knowledge does not come from self-reflection but rather from understanding our cultural condition as intertwined with history. It is this conviction that is so interesting in relation to cultural expressions of life beyond language. If we are so intertwined with history, indeed all our cultural actions and manifestations of life are imbued with historicity, but how are these manifestations interpreted in different historical time periods? And how do these interpretations imply a certain level of subjectivity, as Dilthey claims occurs with the interpretation of historical texts?

II.I The language of architecture

The fascination with language that has dominated the last thirty years of the twentieth century is epitomized by an architecture that has aimed to rescue symbols and signs from architectural history. But referring to history is very different from expressing history, and this is an important distinction to make. The turn to symbols that represent historical architectural motifs has significantly shaped architectural theory and practice of the second half of the twentieth century and is very eloquently embodied in the work of Denise Scott Brown and Robert Venturi. In their influential publications and through their research of the city, the authors championed the idea of architecture as having a communicative linguistic dimension of its own, contrasting architecture that represents with architecture that expresses.[13]

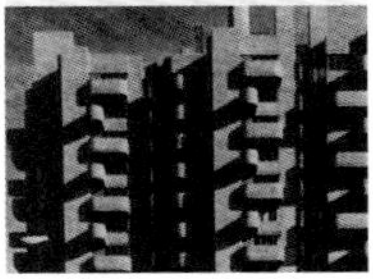

The authors famously categorize architecture under two main headings: "the duck" on one hand and the "decorated shed" on the other. The first case is inspired by a duck-shaped building that aims to communicate something by using what they initially call "symbolic form", and then proceed to call "expressionistic architecture".[14] The second claims to be a banal box-like construction, a shed, on which decoration can be applied: "the decorated shed". To elucidate their point, they compare the image of two buildings, one by Paul Rudolf, and the other by the authors themselves, Denise Scott Brown and Robert Venturi.[15] They criticize Rudolf's work as being "a duck" because of its lack of ornamentation and use of expression to convey the complexities of its building technique. They use it as an example of all that they believe to be wrong with modern architecture of the time, which they see as "impoverished" because of its rejection of the long history of iconography in architecture. They describe their use of architectural elements as being superior because it is reliant on what has come before them, recognizing the history from which it emerges. They do not aim to do anything new with architectural elements; they just have elements represent themselves and refer to their historical lineage in order to communicate their historicity. This distinction being made, however, begs the question: if a building is communicating, what is it saying?

II.II Representational and expressive dimensions

There are many buildings that do not necessarily communicate as the examples of the "duck" and "decorated shed" have illustrated. Some buildings are designed with the very intent to question ingrained assumptions about the past, and aim instead to be expressions of their present, becoming vivid expressions of the time in which they were built. To illustrate this difference, it is productive to pick out two buildings that are similar in type (a single-family home) but very different in terms of what they aim to communicate and their relationship to history: Le Corbusier's Villa Savoye and Scott Brown and Venturi's house, designed for his mother.

Vanna Venturi's house is the embodiment of a representational and semantic approach to architecture, as advocated by the architects. It is emblematic of an architecture that needs to be "read"; it is like a semantic game for architects and critics who can read into the details in order to realize the architects' gestural messages through continual references and playful associations with historic architecture and conventional architectural elements:

the outside form—as represented by the parapeted wall and the gable roof which enclose the complexities and distortions—is simple and consistent: it represents this house's public scale. The front, in its conventional combinations of door, chimney, and gable, creates an almost symbolic image of a house.[16]

This kind of architecture aimed to break away from modernism, perceived to be devoid of historical and referential content. Thus, it used representation to play semantic games with architectural language; reviving elements of past architectural traditions and enhancing the use of convention through representation. In order to appreciate this kind of architectural construct, one has to be educated and instructed specifically on how to read such work. One has to understand the subtext of the "complexity and contradiction" present in a house that is, in the words of the architects, "complex and simple, big and little, open and closed".[17] Architectural space was at the service of an interpretative game that relied mostly on historical references and representation. But one could ask: what is this kind of approach toward history actually telling us about its own historical moment?

Le Corbusier's Villa Savoye can be placed in sharp contrast to the house for Venturi's mother, and, in many ways, it is the type of work that Scott Brown and Venturi were rebelling against. Although both are homes and built only thirty years apart, they communicate radically different things. Le Corbusier's project does not "look like"—or represent—a house in a traditional sense; it does not present itself with recognizable historical references, precisely because its design aimed to surpass historical connotations and convention. Le Corbusier was very much invested in the project of going beyond history. This brings us back to Dilthey and the question of history. Unlike Hegel, for Dilthey, the drive of history is not relegated to the world of ideas, it is a more complex drive which is deeply intertwined with cultural manifestations of life. In his description of "the driving force in history", Dilthey seems to recognize the cultural need to surpass history:

the driving force in history is always something unsatisfactory in a cultural situation. Thus the urge to go beyond it arises.[18]

Le Corbusier was indeed in a very particular cultural situation and had the need to surpass the implied historicity of the architecture that was being built at the time. He wished to be recognized in his own right and to liberate himself from the ways of the past in order to produce something completely new. He was nonetheless responding to history, just not through mimicry. It is therefore much harder to "read" or interpret Villa Savoye as a home and yet it communicates very vividly the philosophy of its time.[19] It cannot be understood at a glance; it needs to be experienced, to be explored in its multiple scales: as an object on the landscape, framing the landscape, as a "machine for living" by the intimate exploration of its spaces through the experience of navigating its interior.[20] It is hard to comprehend immediately. One could argue that in this intelligibility also lies its sense of historicity, and the capacity that non-representational architecture has to innovate and question the history of built architecture, while simultaneously being expressions of their own historical time. Villa Savoye no longer represents a house, rather it expresses a mode of living. It is tied to the time in which it was built and, as such, is a vivid expression of its own historical time.

II.III Social historicity

The notion of representation used in architectural terminology, and as made explicit by Scott Brown and Venturi's writing, is much like Dilthey's notion of interpretation. It refers to the use of architectural elements that refer to something external to themselves and that need to be interpreted by an educated viewer who can decipher what certain motifs are supposed to communicate. It relies on conventional models of what a certain typology is supposed to look like and, as a result, on what it is supposed to communicate: a pitched roof communicates "home" or "homeliness", for example. While these formal and material choices might be used to transmit an expected legibility or satisfy the demands of a client, they limit the potential that architecture has to question the status quo, to uncover novel responses to changing ways of living, of being an expression of its time and, in a sense, being worthy of its own historicity. Indeed, how can we know anything about the time in which the architecture was built, if it refers back to historical architecture that has long passed? It seems that relying on historical motifs is antithetical to a built environment that is expressive of its own time. Architecture that expresses its own historicity does not rely on bygone historical conventions; it focuses on what it can do and what it can express about its own time while still informed by the cultural context in which it emerges. This kind of architecture gives us insight into the social and cultural dimensions of human experience and as such, an objective understanding of its philosophy of history. As Deleuzians would say: it is worthy of its time.[21] Furthermore, and to continue the Deleuzian reference, Dilthey's way of looking at history has an imaginative dimension: history is always in the process of making itself, always in the process of becoming. Unless we arrive at the end of history, we cannot ever have full grasp of the meaning of things.[22]

Architecture in its built form is able to provide a glimpse into a historical era without the need to arrive to "the end of history". The built environment is an end of sorts, even though it goes on living, it does provide us with a frozen temporality of the original historical moment; it is like music frozen in time.[23] Examples of this are the many churches and public projects whose construction spanned so many years that the end result is a material expression of multiple historical periods and construction techniques. The Duomo of Florence is a vivid example of this, with construction spanning almost two hundred years, beginning in the Gothic style and culminating in the Renaissance dome designed by Filippo Brunelleschi, expressive of all the structural innovations and aesthetic breakthroughs of the time.[24] A more recent and still evolving example is the building of the Sagrada Familia in Barcelona by Antoni Gaudí. This building's construction started in 1882 and it is still under construction today.[25] While the formal expression and Gaudí's overall design are maintained, the techniques of construction are so different today that they are inevitably having a repercussion on the cathedral itself, which has provoked contentious arguments between historical purists and those claiming that architecture has to be an expression of its time.

III Non-linguistic expressivity

III.I Historicity in the "posthuman" era

Despite all its insight and richness, Dilthey's work might also be seen as somewhat problematic for a twenty-first-century reader. Dilthey's ontology rests on the separation between the human and natural sciences, emphasizing a dualistic way of understanding the role of humans in the world; exacerbating the dualistic vision of nature and culture that sets "us" against "them" of the non-human natural world. The strict demarcation between the human and natural sciences, which sees nature and culture in opposition to one another, can also be seen as the root of many of our environmental problems. Dilthey sees this duality as a problem, and says so explicitly, but he does not think that the philosophical attempts at resolving it have been fruitful:

> *These philosophical systems are of no use. What we need is to grasp the inner relation of these two worlds in ourselves, how we adopt changing views on the world. Sometimes we feel ourselves to be part of nature—mysterious, instinctive, earthbound ...*[26]

Dilthey does not quite finish this thought, leaving a large gap that contemporary readers must aim to fill. When Dilthey differentiates between the human and the natural, he uses history as the exemplary human science and, curiously, he sees the natural world in a completely different light, with the natural sciences operating at a completely different level, devoid of historicity. We have the benefit of hindsight and can now wonder why Darwin's theory of natural selection did not affect Dilthey's thinking.[27]

Darwin's theory of natural selection can actually be seen as the equivalent of Dilthey's notion of historicity, just from the perspective of natural sciences. Natural selection and evolution are imbued with the idea that nature is intertwined with its past; much like Dilthey claims humans are intertwined with their history. We know that nature and humans are not occupying entirely different worlds, which points to an obvious conclusion that Dilthey and Darwin are claiming very similar things, just doing so from two different vantage points.[28]

The division between the human and the natural was a much-debated topic during Dilthey's time, and it is still contested today. It has become an even more salient concern with the expanded notion and questioning of what it means to be human, given our present condition as tightly intertwined with our technology and mediated environments. It is becoming increasingly difficult to separate the organic from the non-organic algorithms that rule our daily lives. It seems inconceivable to a contemporary reader to uphold a humanistic notion of man as the universal measure of existence, distinct from the natural world, or even distinct from the non-biological world we helped create. Expanding Dilthey's contention of us being intertwined with history with a more Darwinian notion that holds us linked with the environment that sustains us is critical. Much like Darwin's natural selection of the species, our bodies and capacities have evolved with the needs and challenges of the world we inhabit.

While this deviates from Dilthey's perspective, it raises fascinating questions about what it is to be human. Indeed, there is an accruing literature on the "posthuman" condition that sees us not as separate entities but as embedded in our environment in continuum with nature, and also with our technology.[29] Without delving into this area much further, suffice it to say, one can hold onto incredibly suggestive concepts in relation to history without holding onto the dualistic frameworks within which Dilthey is situated.

Dilthey's distinction between the human and the natural sciences is problematic, but his insight into the imaginative dimension of history and the capacity that other disciplines have to shape philosophical discourse is important. While he is not particularly organized in the structure and buildup of his arguments, his work is very rich with new ideas, and the lack of complete closure of his arguments allows for others to get excited about finding new avenues of thought and developing them further, possibly even in a direction that Dilthey might not have cared for. He would, however, have supported the thought that the value of historical work is not just to help us understand the present but also to project new possibilities into the future.

Built structures that surround us and form our urban reality are the products of specific philosophically driven historical processes and, as such, are a material expression of our historicity. Historical knowledge gained through artistic manifestations of life have the capacity to express our historicity in a deeper, more complex, and multifaceted way than historical texts because they involve experience. It is true that experiences will never be identical; indeed, often they are intentionally different, given that architectural spaces are programmed and reprogrammed continuously into different uses, and, as such, they offer different kinds of experiences. There is a fuller sensorial involvement in the experience of architecture than in the experience of texts because of its bodily nature; it requires being embodied and embedded. We do not really need to use all our senses to read, write, and interpret texts; we do not need to have a sense of balance, touch, or smell. However, the experience of our material world requires a complex mode of interpretation, which is multisensorial as well as intellectual.

Endnotes

1 Wilhelm Dilthey, *The Formation of the Historical World in the Human Sciences*. Princeton: Princeton University Press, 2002, p 271.

2 "There is an intrinsic temporality to all understanding." Dilthey being quoted by Richard Palmer in *Hermeneutics*, Evanston, IL: Northwestern University Press, 1969, p 117.

3 Ibid, p 116.

4 For Dilthey, spirit or mind is not an abstract intellectual principle or disembodied behavioral experience, but refers to the individual's life in its concrete cultural-historical context. Dilthey, *The Formation*, p 226.

5 Ibid, p 228.

6 Ibid.

7 He also references music throughout his texts and often applied this to music as well.

8 The word "architecture" is being used in its narrow sense, referring to built architecture.

9 Dilthey, *The Formation*, p 237.

10 Ibid, p 229.

11 Ibid, p 242.

12 Ibid, p 297.

13 *Complexity and Contradiction in Architecture* by Robert Venturi, and *Learning from Las Vegas* by Denise Scott Brown, Robert Venturi, and Steven Izenour. The latter book was actually the result of a research project started by Denise Scott Brown, and later developed collectively by the co-authors and their students from Yale in 1968, where they aimed to put forth an unbiased analysis of this unique American city. Through Scott Brown's research in Las Vegas, they detected the proliferation of icons and symbols seen as exemplary of the communicative dimension of architecture.

14 Scott Brown, Venturi, and Izenour, *Learning from Las Vegas*, p 87.

15 The Crawford Manor by Paul Rudolph and the Guild House by Denise Scott Brown and Venturi are both high-rise apartments for the elderly built in the mid-sixties. The authors claim they are comparing the "image" of the buildings, not the buildings themselves.

16 Venturi, *Complexity and Contradiction in Architecture*, p 118.

17 Ibid, p 118.

18 Dilthey, *The Formation*, p 290.

19 For instance, the emergence of the car with the raised architectural volume to allow for parking, and the fascination for industry with pure forms and mechanic parts.

20 Le Corbusier's slogan words: "A house is a machine for living" (Une maison est une machine à habiter), in *Towards a New Architecture*, Paris: Courier Corporation, 1931.

21 "Philosophy's sole aim is to become worthy of the event." Gilles Deleuze and Félix Guattari, *What is Philosophy?* Translated by Janis Tomlinson. New York: Columbia University Press, 1996, p 160.

22 See Francis Fukuyama, *The End of History and the Last Man*, New York: Simon and Schuster, 2006.

23 This is a reference to Goethe's much quoted "Music is liquid architecture; Architecture is frozen music."

24 The construction of Santa Maria del Fiore began in 1296 in the Gothic style with the design of Arnolfo di Cambio (who already was trying to surpass the Gothic style by avoiding flying buttresses). It was completed with Brunelleschi's innovative double-shelled dome in 1436.

25 For a full understanding of the lineage please see: http://www.sagradafamilia.org/en/history-of-the-temple (accessed December 6, 2020).

26 Dilthey, *The Formation*, p 296.

27 Darwin (1809–1882) and Dilthey (1833–1911) were contemporaries, but I could not find any evidence of Dilthey explicitly knowing Darwin's work.

28 As a Spinozist would claim, indeed they are saying the same thing, because nature and culture are aspects of the same thing, just seen from different perspectives. Much like mind-body, nature-culture are in Spinoza's words "the same substance".

29 See Rosi Braidotti, *The Posthuman*, Cambridge: Polity Press, 2013.

Bibliography

Braidotti, Rosi. *The Posthuman*. Cambridge: Polity Press, 2013.

Carr, David. *Experience and History*. Oxford: Oxford University Press, 2014.

Danto, Arthur. "Substantive and Analytic Philosophy of History" in *Analytical Philosophy of History*. Michigan: University Press, 2006.

De Balzac, Honoré. *The Quest of The Absolute*. Cambridgeshire: Dedalus Ltd, 2005.

Deleuze, Gilles and Félix Guattari. *What is Philosophy?* Translated by Janis Tomlinson. New York: Columbia University Press, 1996.

Dilthey, Wilhelm. *The Formation of the Historical World in the Human Sciences*. Princeton: Princeton University Press, 2010.

Fukuyama, Francis. *The End of History and the Last Man*. New York: Simon and Schuster, 2006.

Harries, Karsten. *The Ethical Function of Architecture*. Cambridge, MA: MIT Press, 1997.

Hegel, G.W.F. *Introduction to the Philosophy of History*. Translated by Leo Rauch. London: Hackett Publishing Company, Inc., 1998.

Le Corbusier. *Towards a New Architecture*. Paris: Courier Corporation, 1931.

Palmer, Richard. *Hermeneutics*. Evanston, IL: Northwestern University Press, 1969.

Scott Brown, Denise, Robert Venturi, Steven Izenour. *Learning from Las Vegas*. Cambridge, MA, and London: MIT Press, 1998.

Venturi, Robert. *Complexity and Contradiction in Architecture*. New York: Museum of Modern Art Press, 1966.

Illustrations

The Duck and the decorated shed, p 91. Denise Scott-Brown, Robert Venturi, and Steven Izenour.

Learning from Las Vegas, p 92. *Learning from Las Vegas*. Cambridge, MA, and London: MIT Press, 1998, pp 88–89 and pp 94–95.

House for Vanna Venturi, p 92. Robert Venturi, *Complexity and Contradiction in Architecture*, p 119.

Le Corbusier's Villa Savoye, p 92. Found on designboom.com.

piazza ceramica

2011

Piazza Ceramica was the winner of the international competition for the design of a pavilion for Ceramics of Italy's largest annual event. Designed as a 3D puzzle of parts that are assembled and disassembled for reuse, it was the longest-running pavilion—the parts were brought to life for five consecutive years.

The formal gesture emerged from the idea of gently lifting the opposite corners of the rectangular site, allowing the form to elegantly house the required program elements while maintaining a spacious, articulated surface above, for people to gather. Gentle plaza-like steps rise up from the platform to form mounds at opposite ends of the plaza, becoming seating surfaces as it steepens.

In an attempt to counter preconceived notions of tile as a rigidly orthogonal material, the project uses Italian handcraft with water-jet technologies to demonstrate the potential of tile with a fluid expression. The open gathering plaza and eating spaces suggest different program zones with gradient shades of green; the darker greens are slower areas where furniture is arranged for people to linger, while the white areas in-between suggest flow and access to service areas. The curved surfaces for the risers are achieved using mosaic ceramic tile left ungrouted to allow for disassembly and repacking as a flat surface for storage and future re-use.

Strongly inspired by the many hours Eva and Ian spent sitting on piazza steps as high-school students in Rome, where they met, the design is an inviting open public space articulated with gradual steps that invite social gatherings and casual interactions. The formal complexity of the pavilion is achieved with a simple system of fabrication and precise digitally generated components. The cantilevering structure that supports the tiled mounds is a gridshell of CNC cut-plywood ribs designed to be flat-packed and assembled onsite as a three-dimensional puzzle piece. As a gridshell structure, it derives its strength from double curvature, while the grid assembly provides precision. Similarly, tiles were water-jet cut to ensure precise joinery and preset off-site into modular components for fast on-site assembly.

This project was designed with the belief that architecture itself can be a vivid materialization of cultural histories, without the use of language. Colors are, of course, a strong symbology of Italian culture, but the design aims to showcase a way of life, a form of gathering around food and drink that tells us more about the culture that inspires it.

4700
4600

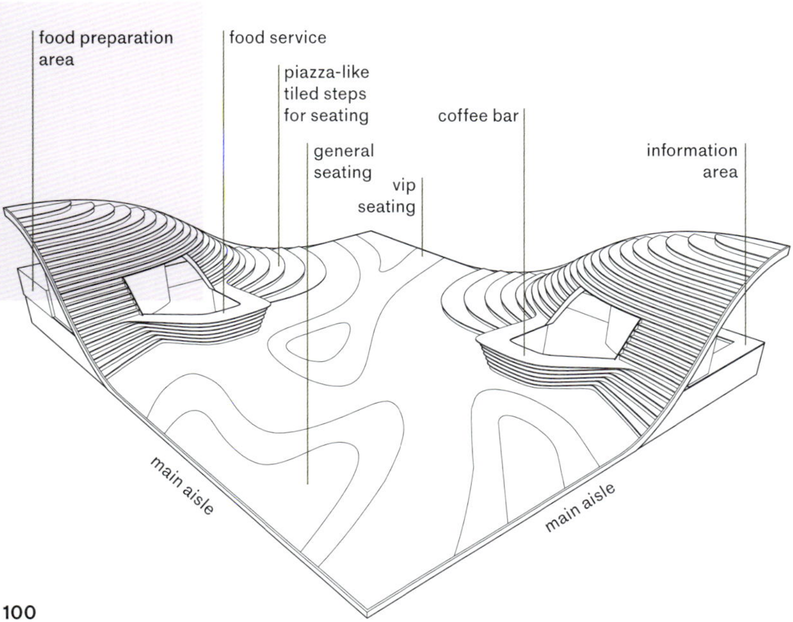
food preparation area
food service
piazza-like tiled steps for seating
coffee bar
general seating
information area
vip seating
main aisle
main aisle

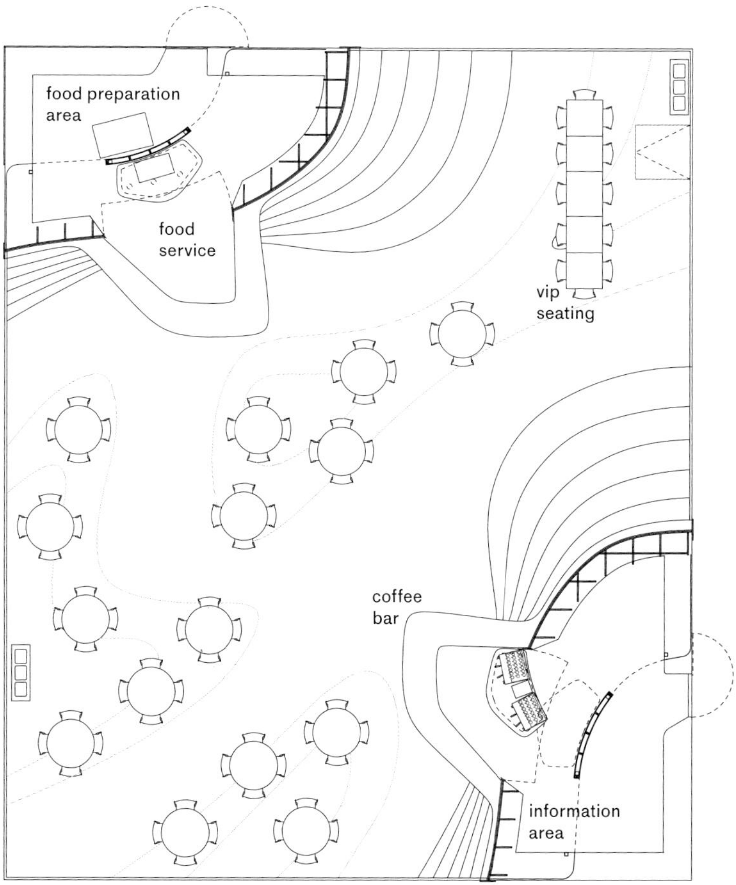

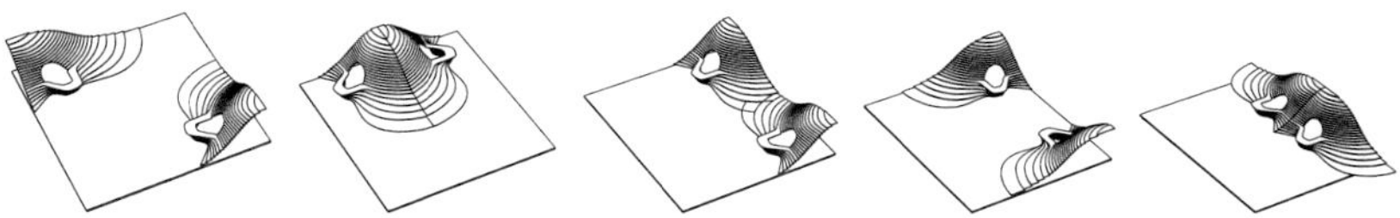

possible alternate configurations

Project data

- **Location** Orlando, Florida
- **Design** Eva Perez de Vega + Ian Gordon
- **Organization** Ceramics of Italy
- **US representative** Novita PR
- **Structural Consultant** Zak Kostura, ARUP
- **Construction** A&M Production
- **Water-jet cutting** Stratos

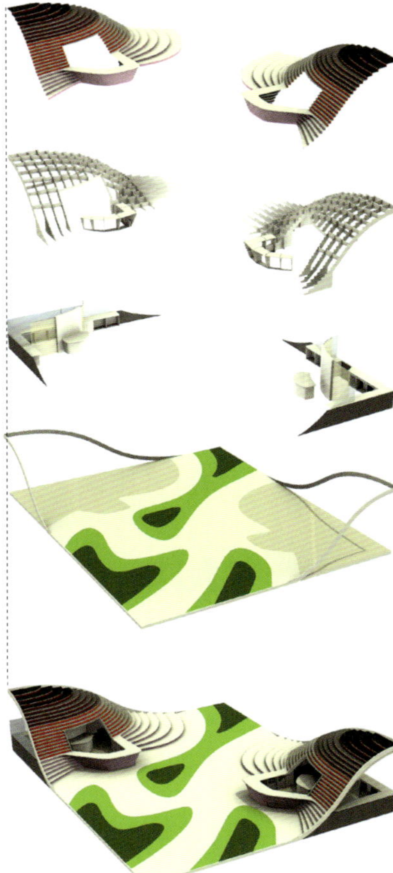

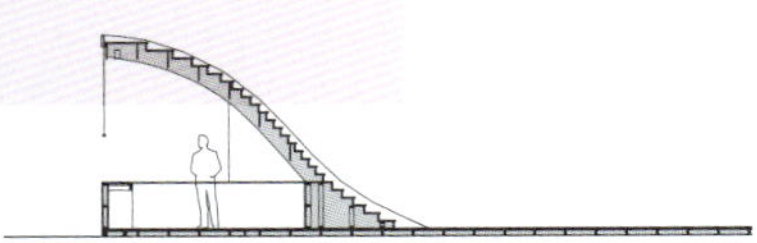

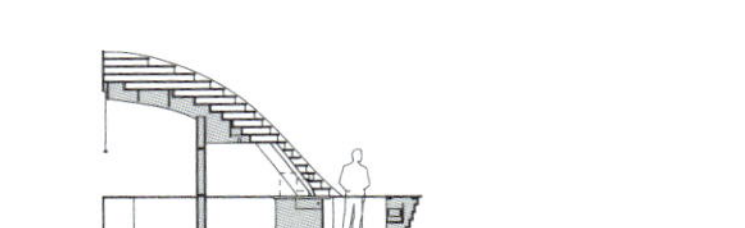

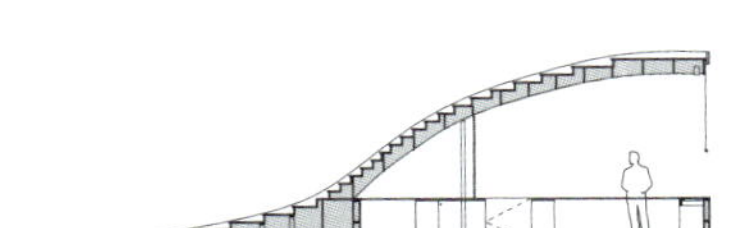

daegu public library

2012

The Daegu Public library plays a critical role in reinforcing the local community by providing free access to information through the open oculi and small "info pods" scattered in the landscape. It also provides spaces for human community events such as festivals, fashion shows, weddings, lectures, and exhibitions as well as providing a landscaped green roof and garden spaces on the ground for nonhuman communities of plants and animals to thrive.

Traditionally used for lending books and providing study spaces, a public library today must do so much more; it must become a central gathering space that exchanges and absorbs information from the city it is located in. A critical part of the design is to make the library feel as open and porous as possible. Visitors are welcomed to the main entry through the landscaped paths, arriving at the open plaza, which opens onto the multifunctional room, or main "oculus", on the entry facade. This space can be fully opened for events that require large gatherings such as concerts and screenings which spill out into the city, or it can be fully enclosed for a more controlled environment. The ground floor is an open, dynamic, and spacious area where visitors can easily access the information portal arranged along the glass facade.

The formal organization for the Library comes from the idea of pinching the floor slabs together, similar to how pastry chefs pinch dough. The oculi are the conceptual and literal organizing idea for the library. The structure uses a proprietary concrete slab system with voids with the slab to drastically reduce the amount of concrete used, the overall weight of the building, and the CO2 emissions involved in the production. To foster an ecological approach, the library harnesses solar light for electrical needs and has a water filtration system that collects water on the green roof, used for the park and street irrigation.

To offer more opportunities for the community to gather, we extended the landscape and provided a Library Park with playgrounds, sport facilities, and heavily planted zones to invite nonhuman species. Recognizing that we are not in a dualistic framework where the "natural" and the "human" are distinct, the library bleeds outward with scattered "pods" that provide open-air reading opportunities and equitable access to information through decentralized portals connected to all online library materials.

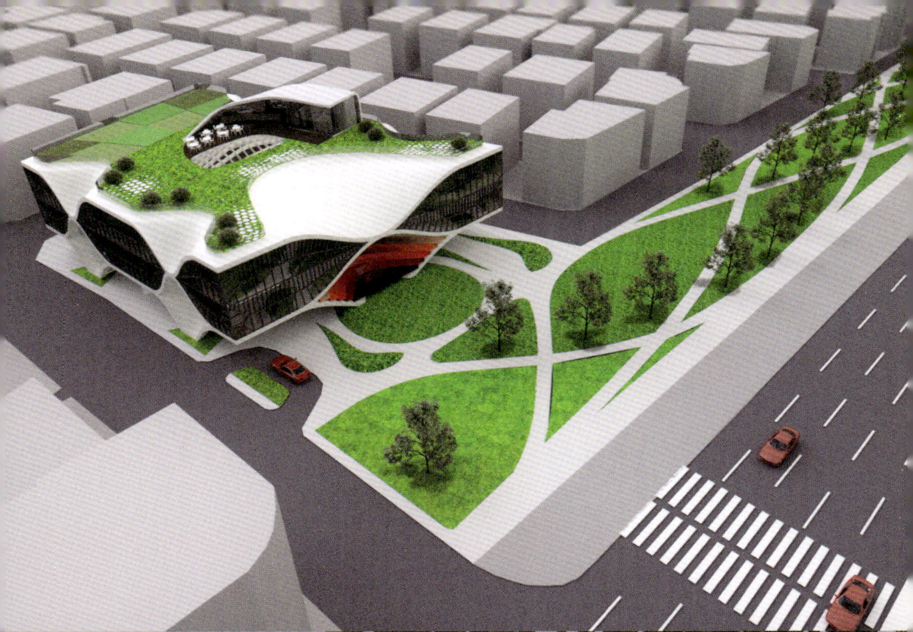

Project data

- **Location** Daegu Gosan, South Korea
- **Design** Eva Perez de Vega + Ian Gordon
- **Facade studies** Yotam Ben-Hur
- **Organization** Daegu Metropolitan City Suseong-gu Office

second floor

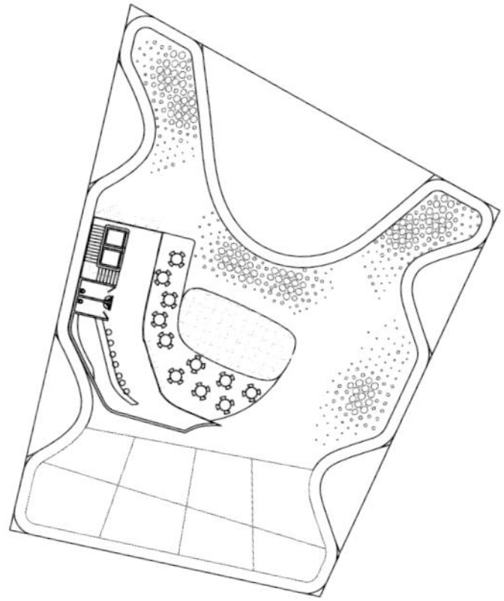

third floor

ground floor

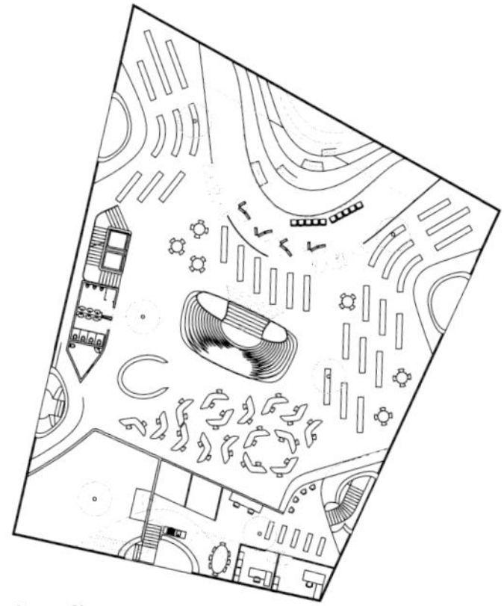

first floor

dubrovnik behind the city urban development

2011

This project generates new gathering areas and improved connectivity for the residents of Dubrovnik, a historic site with emerging needs as a contemporary city. The proposal aims to simultaneously support the essential tourism industry while also enhancing local ecologies for the flourishing of nonhuman life. It is inspired by the unique location of the site as an outer belt to the Roman walls that both protects and frames history, while also injecting the city with new life and future potential.

As a World Heritage Site, the city attracts many tourists, but it must also respond to the changing needs of its inhabitants and a re-establishment of ecologies that the built environment often replaces. The new design provides much-needed services, decongestion, and ecological restoration, as well as new recreational and cultural facilities linked by different modes of alternative transportation, which include a carbon-neutral solar-powered sky train, bike-share system with new facilities for parking and renting, and numerous scenic pedestrian pathways.

The development is imagined as a green urban ribbon embedded with varying qualities and characteristics. It is formed by four distinct ecological zones organized around the outer wall structure that embraces the city center. The urban intervention follows a vertical and horizontal strategy; the vertical strategy allows for a layered organization of modes of transport and programmed spaces that harness the dramatic depth of the site and recognize the layers of its geological history; the horizontal strategy maximizes the continuity of green planted surfaces, program, and multi-species networks.

A key principle for the development of this phased urban proposal is the notion of striations, horizontal bands that reveal layers of geological history. In it one can perceive the manifestation of interconnected human and nonhuman life and lived experiences. The architecture requires us to reflect on what has passed in order to project something new into a more environmentally aware future.

Project data

- **Location** Dubrovnik, Croatia
- **Design** Eva Perez de Vega + Ian Gordon
- **Assistant** Aviva Novick
- **Organization** European Hrvatska, Ministry of Environmental Protection, Physical Planning and Construction

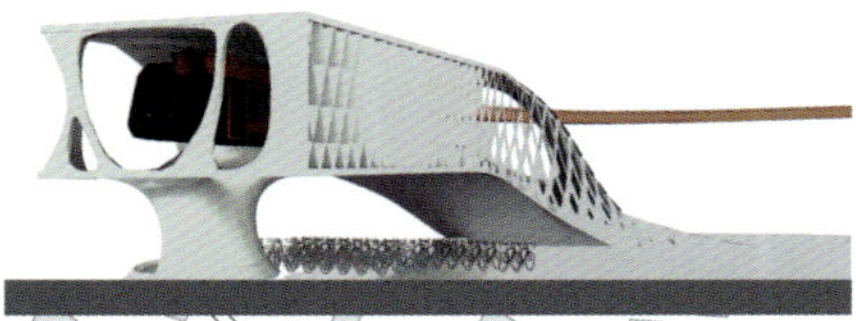

01 **ZONE A**: city services/pile gate
02 **ZONE B**: woodlands
03 **ZONE C**: event spaces/buza gate
04 **ZONE D**: arts and recreation /ploce gate

highbridge museum in the clouds

2010

High Bridge, the oldest bridge in New York City, opened as part of the Croton Aqueduct in 1848 but was later substituted by a single 140-foot-long steel arch spanning over the Harlem River to improve boat navigation. Our project continues the engineering prowess that is part of the bridge's history through a suspended cloud-like structure, which reinvests the existing infrastructure with new cultural and recreational possibilities centered around the notion of multi-species gathering and coexistence.

From below, the project creates an image of dramatic infrastructure surrounded by clouds in the sky; a deterritorialized zone suspended above the city. From within, the cloud produces moments of the Sublime, where the user experiences a sense of extreme suspended formlessness. The transparency of the structural bands allows the city to view activity within the cloud, and engenders new plant life to inspire connections between the neighborhood people and the bird species migrating through this region.

The uncanny feeling of suspension and formlessness exacerbated by the physical detachment from land and water is counteracted by the powerful presence of the aqueduct infrastructure. Rather than demolishing what is seen as a system that no longer functions, our proposal reveals and repairs it, making it become the protagonist of the story by exposing the water main that contributed to the formation and expansion of New York City. This is not merely a symbolic gesture; the aqueduct is put back into service to supply water for nonhuman life found within the cloud topology.

The cloud-like structure is supported by a structural tubular ribbon at the top level of the bridge from which a topography of stairs and platforms is suspended. This main ribbon is the shell that houses the new Croton Aqueduct Museum, creating a continuous visual dialogue with the Highbridge water main. The linear museum typology becomes a unique network of spaces that captures the expansiveness of the Croton water system and the technical complexity of the Croton infrastructure project.

The cloud form affords a multiplicity of unforeseen programmatic uses and novel social exchanges that include nonhuman life, and cannot be glanced at and understood—it needs to be experienced and explored in its multiple scales.

The transparency of the form allows for a visual and physical reassessment of the city and the bridge from within it, but most importantly, a connection and a recognition of the infrastructural histories that made the city possible.

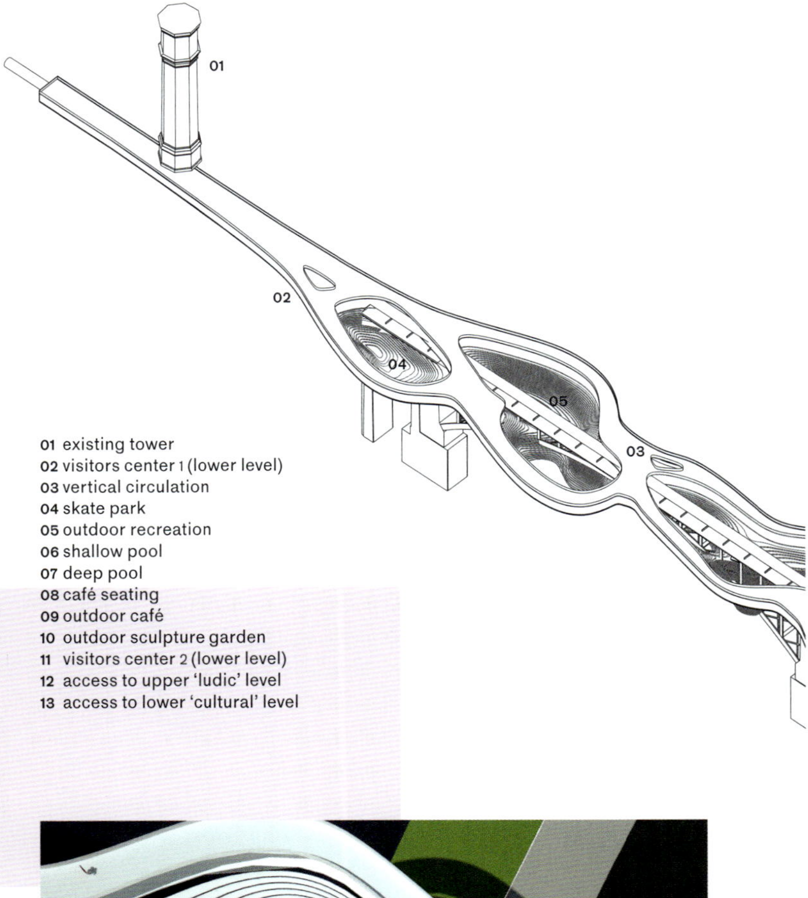

01 existing tower
02 visitors center 1 (lower level)
03 vertical circulation
04 skate park
05 outdoor recreation
06 shallow pool
07 deep pool
08 café seating
09 outdoor café
10 outdoor sculpture garden
11 visitors center 2 (lower level)
12 access to upper 'ludic' level
13 access to lower 'cultural' level

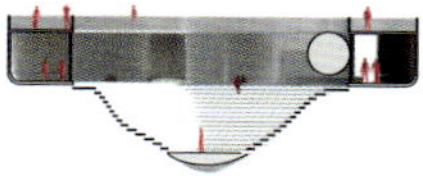

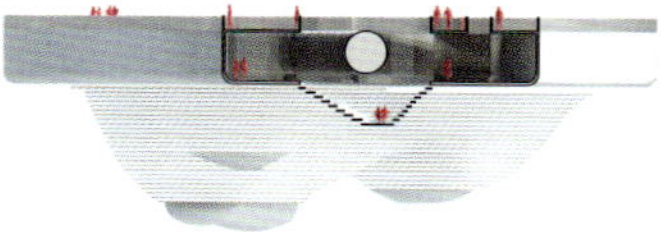

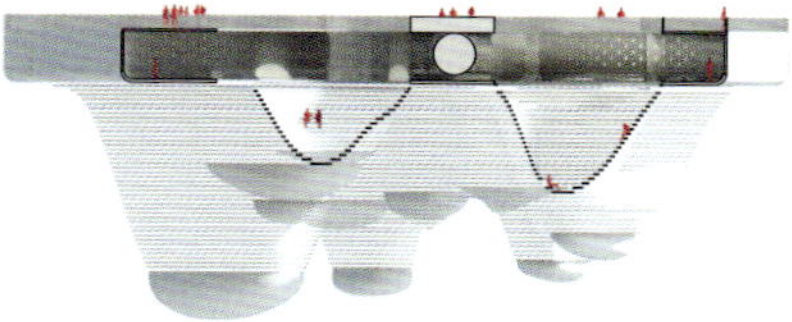

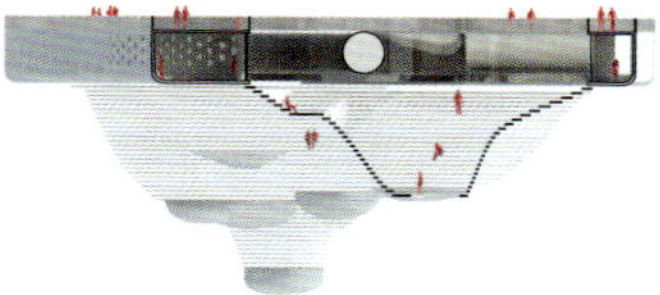

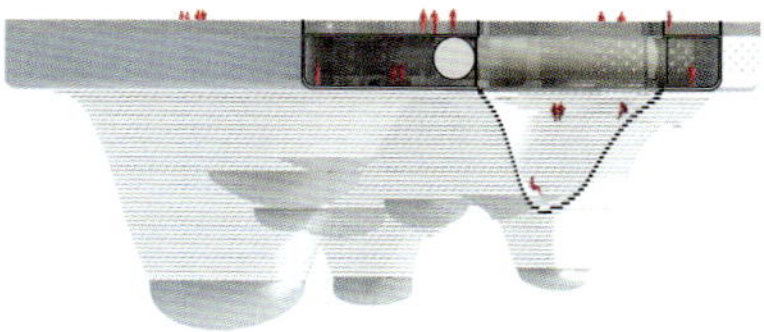

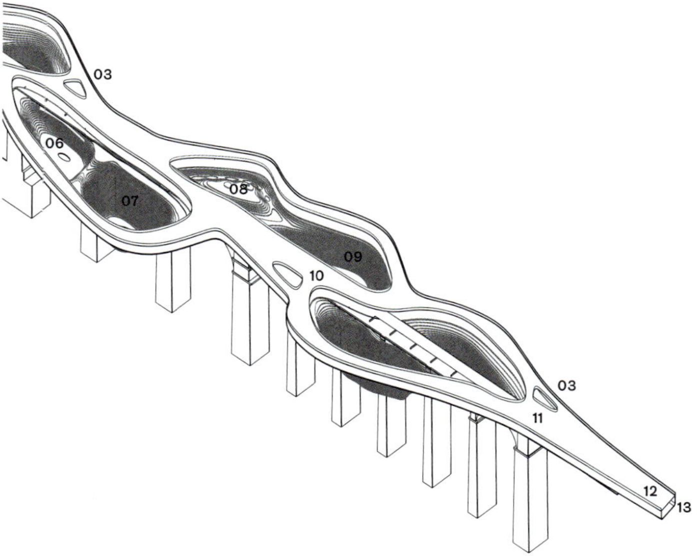
03
06
07
08
09
10
03
11
12
13

Project data

- **Location** The Bronx, New York City
- **Design** Eva Perez de Vega + Ian Gordon
- **Organization** Emerging New York Architects Committee (ENYA), AIA NY Chapter

OPPOSITE Speculatively recreated without human visitors, this proposal allows for a flourishing of nonhuman ecosystems of land and air. The underbelly of the bridge would be home to the northern long-eared bat, now threatened, and the endangered red fox could find refuge at the base of the bridge, while the cloud-like structure would house a multitude of bio-life. We speculate that species now extinct would re-emerge as augmented versions of themselves, as can be seen in the illustration with the mastodons—mythical New York creatures—drinking by the riverbank and the passenger pigeon, which would use the surface as a resting spot during migration.

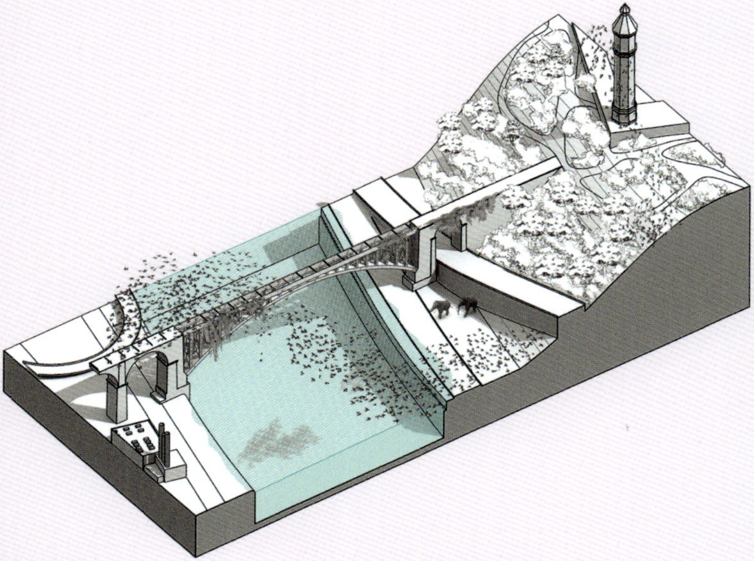

2050 alternative

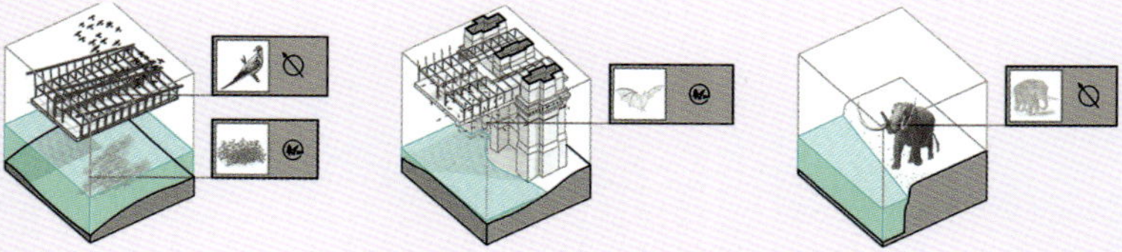

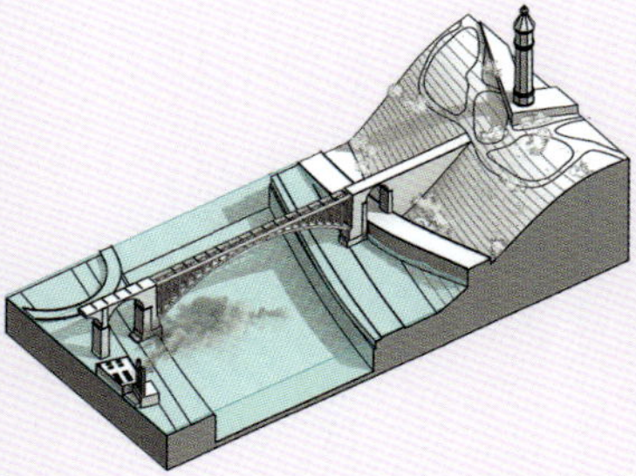

2050

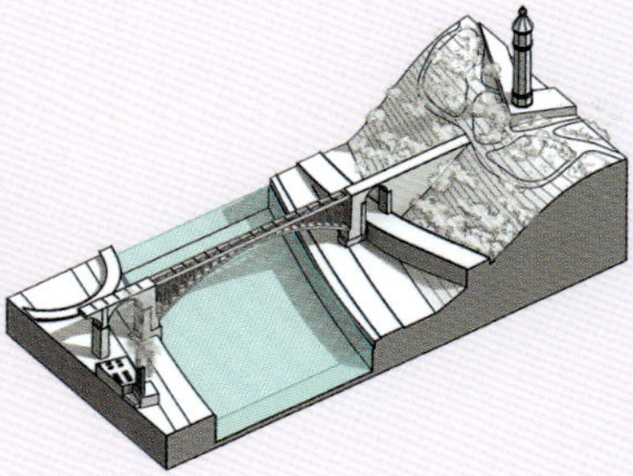

present

mag.net
performance
installation

nuages
performance
installation

fluid adagio
public plaza

perform

south street
seaport
museum

In the discipline and practice of architecture, there is a codified relationship between drawing and building. But what is the nature of this relationship? While there are some similarities between architectural representation and pictorial representation, the relationship drawing-to-building does not seem to be one that relies on resemblance or identical ontology, as some would claim photography does with the object being photographed. Nor is it entirely abstract or notational like music, in which the score and the musical outcome of that score being performed bear no likeness. The case of architecture seems to be different from that of music and different from other visual practices such as photography, painting, and sculpture.

I The mixed case of architecture

I.I Allographic and autographic practices: the role of notation

The distinction made by philosopher Nelson Goodman in his seminal work *Languages of Art* between practices understood as being autographic versus those that are allographic is of particular interest when tackling architecture, understood as an artistic practice.[1] According to Goodman, autographic arts are those that rely on the direct contact of the author with the artwork for its authenticity. This is the case of some visual arts such as painting and sculpture, where the uniqueness of the art piece is as important as the knowledge of its history and particular conditions of production. Any reproduction of a work of art from the autographic group would be considered a replica or copy, and thus not authentic.

At the other end of the spectrum are artistic practices with outcomes where the uniqueness of the piece does not matter, because it can exist in many copies and does not rely on the direct intervention of the author for its production. This is the case for music, poetry, dance, and theater, and is what Goodman calls the allographic arts.[2] The notion of authenticity acquires a different meaning in allographic arts, because they are capable of being produced at a distance from the author. Music is a particularly clear case of an allographic art because, despite differences that may occur in a performance, every performance of a particular music composition will count as an authentic instance of that work.[3] So, the uniqueness that is so important in autographic becomes somewhat irrelevant in the case of allographic arts. The production of a piece from a practice that is allographic relies on something other than the hand of the author of the piece; it relies on notation:

> *an art seems to be allographic just insofar as it is amenable to notation, [...] Amenability to notation depends upon a precedent practice that*

develops only if works of the art in question are commonly either ephemeral or not producible by one person.[4]

For Goodman, the distinction between autographic and allographic arts allows for a rigorous discussion on notation. The classification of painting, sculpture, poetry, dance,[5] and theater as allographic seem to be quite uncontroversial for Goodman, but when he comes to architecture, unique complications emerge that put the clarity of the distinction between allographic and autographic arts into question.

I.II Score, sketch, script, and digital-analog modes of representation

Goodman seems to suggest that the relationship between the notational system of architecture (drawings) and its production (building) is not the same as the relationship that other allographic practices have between their notational system and the instantiation of their production. He points to this as being a reason because architecture is not ephemeral like the other arts of dance and theater and music; once a building is built it is there and exists independently of the drawings that were used to make it. Furthermore, architecture is a mixed case, because the modes of representation used are a combination of different kinds of representational techniques, which include the discursive as well as the pictorial.[6]

An architectural plan has this mixed status because it is often a combination of graphic representation, in form of lines and hatches, and non-graphic representation such as dimensions, in the form of numbers, and specifications, in the form of text.

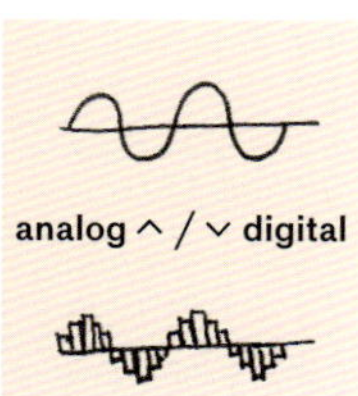

Goodman classifies an architectural plan using three key terms: a score, a sketch, and a script. Even though a score refers to music, a sketch refers to painting, and a script to literary arts, these terms are expanded to include any notational system:

Architectural representations seem to be a combination of the pictorial, in the form of a sketch, and the discursive, as a script, but Goodman claims that:

although a drawing often counts as a sketch, and a measurement in numerals as a script, the particular selection of drawing and numerals in an architectural plan counts as a digital diagram and a score.[7]

But what does he mean by "digital diagram"? It clearly has nothing to do with producing something aided by a computer as is commonly associated by the term. Goodman relates the digital–analog distinction to the notions of density and differentiation;[8] digital systems are distinguished by being differentiated while analog ones are dense.[9] The density of analog systems refers to the notion of continuous variation, in such a way that, given any two marks, there is always a possible third character between them. By contrast, digital systems are always differentiated and have a precise reading of what the representation refers to. Thus, digital representation is notational and analog representation is non-notational.

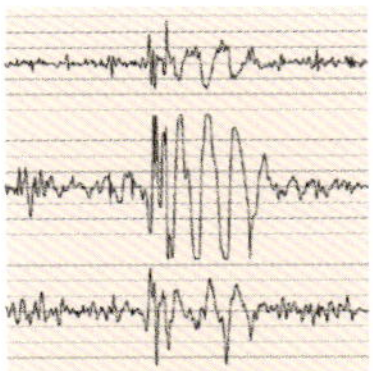

purely analog

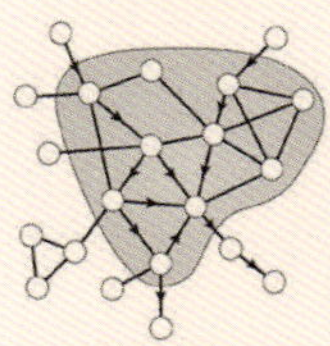

purely digital

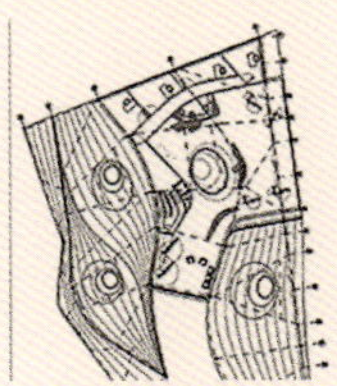

mixed status

A good visual example is a digital and analog clock, where the hour and minute hands in an analog clock are always in a state of motion, and readings from it will always be ambiguous and open to interpretation. While on a digital clock there is always a definite precise time, there is no ambiguity

I.III Diagrams and models

Architectural drawings are both notational and non-notational, digital and analog, insofar as they combine both pictorial representations (sketch) and annotations in text (script) and numerals, yet Goodman claims plans are more akin to being classified as a “digital diagram”.[10] But what does he mean by ‘diagram’?

Diagrams are not by definition either digital or analog. A seismograph would be a case of a purely analog diagram because its reading is not reliant on any notational system, its lines are the result of the motion of the earth and can be understood without added notation. A purely digital example would be that of a topological diagram, which relies on a notational system. In many cases, diagrams can hold a mixed status. For instance, ordinary road maps are a mixed case, containing both analog and digital elements. Most architectural drawings will also have this mixed condition of being both analog and digital, because there will be some sort of spatial quality that can be understood without the use of any notational device, but there are also symbols and conventions of drawing that may not be internal to the drawing itself. These either rely on shared conventions or a specified indexical system on the drawing.

Models are diagrams that tend to have more than one dimension and could have moving parts.[11] Certainly, architectural models are three-dimensional and often can be taken apart or have liftable components that allow the viewer to see inside the space for example. An architectural model is analog with respect to spatial dimensions, but if chipboard is used to denote concrete walls, and acrylic to show glass, then it is digital with respect to its materials, because the materials used for the models are standing in for the actual materials—they are symbolically representing them.

Architectural representation performs as a "diagram" in that it has this mixed status of being at once digital, hence notational, but also analog, pictorial, akin to painting and thus non-notational. This is one of the main reasons Goodman gives for architecture being a mixed case; its representation can be notational and non-notational, digital and analog.

From the diagram below, we see how classical conceptions of painting and photography are representations of things that are already in the world (P2: representation ß world), while architectural representations are usually of something yet to be realized. (A1: notation à instantiation).

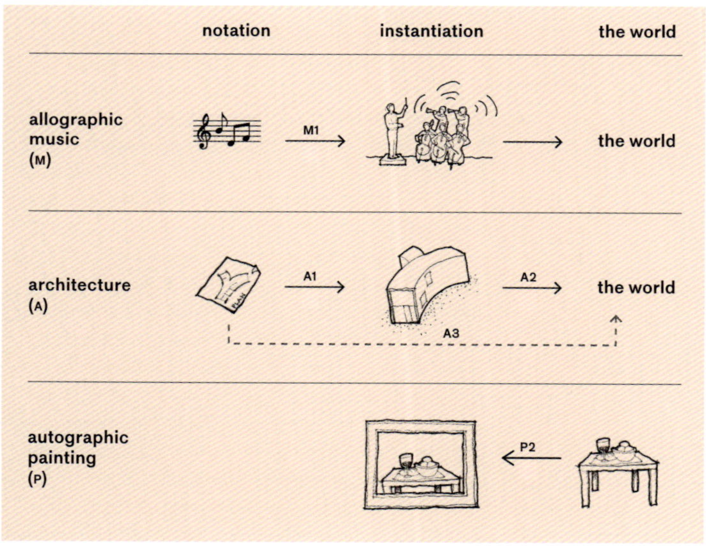

It is from this point, using the above diagram as a road map, that architecture's mixed status can be elaborated on, by exploring the relationship that Goodman mentions but does not develop further, namely between the architectural drawing (what Goodman calls "notational language") and the building (Goodman's "particular production") in architecture;[12] as well as a relationship which is unique to architecture—the relationship between the notation and reality or the world (A3: notation à world).

II Drawing and building

> *"Architects don't make buildings, they make drawings of buildings."*[13]

While architecture is understood as the art and science of building, architects often find themselves removed from the actual act of construction. This is much like a composer, who may be removed from the performance of the piece composed. Even temporally, the work of architects and composers may be instantiated outside of their own lifetime.[14] This is not the case with other pictorial practices such as painting or photography. These practices require the direct involvement of the author as well as "a world" from which they are drawing inspiration to produce their work.

II.I Is drawing to building like score is to music?

The main element that distinguishes an autographic from allographic artistic practice is the existence of a notational system, as well as the direct or indirect involvement of the author in its production.[15] In addition, uniqueness and authenticity, which are important in autographic works, are not relevant in allographic ones.

Architectural work has a close affinity with music because "architectural and musical works, unlike paintings or plays or novels, are seldom descriptive or representational".[16] Indeed, architecture and music do not depict reality, as one could say painting and sculpture have traditionally.[17] Architectural notations, like musical scores, are artifacts that can be decoded, read, according to shared conventions in order to affect reality by creating something that was not there before. Like music, it is a set of instructions for realizing another artifact. Architectural and musical notation are generative in this way because they create new things; a score music; architectural drawings help produce a built artifact.

While it is indeed the case that there are some affinities, the relationship between drawing and building in architecture is not like the one between a score and a performance. For the production of allographic arts such as music, dance, and theater, the notation always needs to be performed in order to exist, while in architecture the production of its notation (the building via the drawings) only needs to happen once and then it exists and is appreciated independently of the existence of its notation. Once built, architecture does not rely on the drawings to exist in the way a musical performance may rely on the score to exist.

This is one way that the relationship between music and its production is different from that of architecture; it does not need to be built in order to be considered architecture, it can exist solely in its representations. One could argue that architectural representations—drawings—often become ends in themselves; a drawing can detach itself from the represented object to become an artifact in its own right, much like a painting. In these cases, it is no less architecture, whether it has been built or not, but its history of production does become important.

Architectural representation is one of the first places where ideological changes manifest themselves. If we look at the drawings of Le Corbusier, for example, for the Carpenter Center, the relationship between drawing and building often exceeds their purely notational function, because drawing does more than just act as a codified instrument for the construction of the building. These drawings show things beyond the utility of what is represented; it illustrated Le Corbusier's theoretical stance; the ramp and column grid are not mere utilitarian elements to get places without steps or support the structure, they are the spatial organizers, which speak to movement and the change in perception through that movement; it is about the experiences that the architect anticipates a user having. This is an example of an unbuilt project that is nonetheless considered architecture. Another example is the work of Giovanni Battista Piranesi, which is mostly unbuilt, but has nonetheless advanced the discipline via the representational tools at the disposal of the architect.[18]

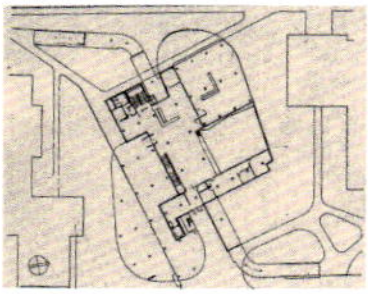

Architect and author Stan Allen is critical of those who claim that the true power of architecture lies in the completed built artifact (a view which he labels as "conservative") as well as those who claim that architecture's real capacity lies in drawings and representations which remain uncontaminated by the compromises of construction (this he labels the "experimental" view).[19] Indeed, some might argue that built architecture is always plagued with the limitations of time, cost, and gravity, which affect the built artifact but do not affect the architectural representations of it. Allen claims that the relationship between the two is what will reveal the capacity that architecture has to intervene productively in the world, but that it is a paradoxical and counterintuitive relationship:

> *Paradoxically, the dry, unemotional form of notation, which makes no attempt to approach reality through resemblance, is better able to anticipate the complexity and unpredictability of the real.*[20]

The distinction between allographic and autographic practices made by Goodman points to the paradoxical character of the relationship between drawing and building. I agree with Stan Allen's contention that for the advancement of the profession there is a demand for drawings to be abstract and far removed from the complications of the real in order to have a productive and transformative effect on reality. I would also contend that drawings have an effect on reality whether it gets built or not. Indeed, as

Goodman says, to assume notation to be an instrumental aid to production is to miss the fundamental theoretical role of notation.[21] Similarly, to assume that drawing is an instrumental aid to the production of the built is to miss the fundamental theoretical role of drawings and their capacity to advance the practice of architecture.

II.II Architecture as allographic

If we take the looser definition and understanding of allographic and autographic, in that architectural drawings use shared conventions, then architecture does seem to have a "reasonably appropriate notational system" and can be said to be allographic. In addition, it shares the allographic quality of being able to be produced at a distance from the author.

If architecture were an allographic artform, we should be comfortable claiming that every instance of certain drawings will produce the same building. However, it is difficult to disassociate buildings with a certain level of uniqueness and notion of authenticity. Using plans designed in one time period to build at a different time period seems to be problematic. If we imagine a developer taking the plans for the Empire State Building and rebuilding it exactly as it is in New York but say in Newark, we would most likely all agree that the authentic one is in New York. Similarly, all the replicas of famous buildings that we can find in Las Vegas are just that: replicas. This is because the history of production is critically important in the case of these buildings. The Eiffel Tower was significant because it used very novel technology of construction with iron; it defied what was thought to be possible, which is not the case of the replica made for the "Paris" hotel of Las Vegas. The recently completed redevelopment of the southern tip of Roosevelt Island is another example of this. It was completed using the plans that Louis Kahn had produced prior to his death in 1974. These plans were never used to build anything else, so this is a genuine instantiation of these plans. Nevertheless, it seems wrong to use them thirty years later, when the island and the surrounding city have developed into something very different from what they were at the time of the plans' inception.[22]

Most works of architecture have a historic specificity, and a site specificity, that makes the history of production essential to their identification. They are not like music, which can be instantiated at different time periods without affecting the authenticity of the composition. In this sense they are unique and closer to an autographic artform. Indeed, it seems that the architectural works we would call autographic are precisely those buildings we regard as works of art. Building a bank with a floor plan, which is similar to that of the Pantheon, does not produce architecture as a work of art, just a crude replica. So, it is not a question of whether architecture is allographic when replicated, but whether architecture is considered an artistic practice.[23]

No matter how notational the architectural drawings might be, the history of production, uniqueness, and authenticity is important in architecture understood as an artistic practice. Does this make architecture autographic? Or should we consider architecture as allographic when it is not built and exists just in its representation, but becomes autographic when built? Indeed, some have gone so far as to claim that architecture is allographic in the "plan stage" but autographic in the "built stage".[24] While architectural drawings always have some contact with instrumentality, they are not merely a means for the built. It is the very notational quality of drawings—their abstraction and lack of resemblance to reality—that allows them to "work on reality from a distance".[25]

II.III Architecture and pictorial practices

In architecture, the development of perspective during the Renaissance emerged as a particular mode of representing architecture. Drawings built in perspective produce a knowledge that is different from paraline drawings such as axonometrics, which preserve the relationships that objects have to each other in a way that is measurable. In orthographic and paraline projection, for example, physical properties of the object must be maintained, as they are, not as they appear to the naked eye; parallel lines in the object must be parallel in the drawing, for instance, even though they appear to the eye to meet at a point, so we may perceive distance. Indeed, one of the hardest things for students learning these drawing techniques is to not confuse what they see (perspective) with what they know (orthographic or paraline) of the object.

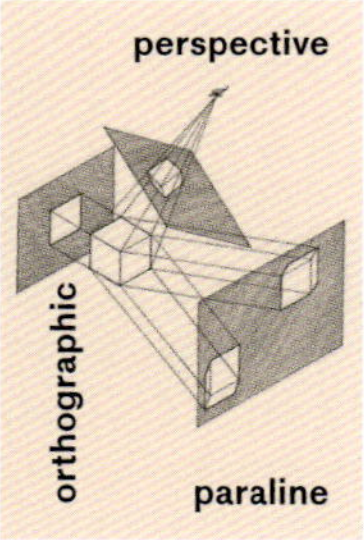

Perspective is the drawing technique that most closely resembles the way humans perceive: things that are further away appear to be smaller, and parallel lines in the world will appear to meet at a vanishing point in a perspectival representation. What we see is actually a distortion of reality that allows us to perceive distance; perspective is a distortion of reality. Perspective is not just a technique of drawing, it also puts the subject at the center of representation, which goes hand in hand with the shift of ideology that marked most of the artwork that was produced in the Renaissance period. Usually shown with the subject's static eye at the center, and perspectival effects unfolding out of it. One could argue that perspective not only affected architectural representation, it also affected architectural production—a way of generating, thinking about, and imagining architecture. It is in this way that architectural representation is generative; it is able to produce new ways of imagining architecture and new realities.[26]

In architectural drawings, perspective is used mostly for renderings which are most similar to pictorial representations.[27] Renderings aim to show how the building would appear once built; to show a building in its context, affected by environmental factors, the sun, wind, and by people moving in and around it.[28] They aim to give a glimpse into how the building might be experienced, and how the material selection might actually look. But while resemblance is important in renderings, the pursuit for realism in an architectural rendering is not uncontroversial. It certainly seems to be the aim behind renderings made for developers or real-estate companies where the goal is to make the look of the representation as realistic and as appealing as possible for commercial purposes.[29] However, the value of the highly realistic architectural rendering for the discipline itself is highly contested, especially in architectural education.

The ability to produce highly realistic renderings is enabled by computer-aided rendering techniques. Prior to the computer, renderings were done by hand using colored pencils and techniques at the disposal of the hand of the renderer; a skilled renderer could produce a more or less realistic depiction of the building in context, but these depictions would never be confused with the real building, in the way a computer-generated rendering might be confused with a photograph of the completed work. Indeed, prior to the computer, the notion of realism in a rendering was similar to the notion of realism in painting prior to photography; it was a goal for some artists, but rarely would we claim there to be an identical ontology between the representation and reality.

There is a compelling parallel between what the invention of photography has done to painting with what the invention and use of the computer has done to architecture. This ties into the debate around mechanically reproduced artwork, and the observations made by Walter Benjamin and others on what mechanical reproduction, via photography and other means, has done to artforms such as painting.

III Architecture in the age of digital (re)production

Walter Benjamin's pivotal text *Art in the Age of Mechanical Reproduction* aimed to question the effect mechanical reproducibility has on artforms themselves. His contention is that mechanical reproducibility, enabled by the invention of photography and film, caused a real crisis and breakage in traditional artforms, such as painting and sculpture.

In architecture, a similar question has been in the air, ever since the computer was introduced as a means to produce and reproduce drawings. There is a belief that digital production is causing a crisis in architecture and the tradition of drawing. Thus, to summarize Benjamin's main contention in a question: what is the effect of mechanically reproduced artwork on the artwork itself? In order to address a similar question: what is the effect of digitally produced architecture on the architecture that is produced?

III.I Architectural representation and photography

In photography, the common-sense view is that the photograph reproduces what is out in the real world; the relationship between the representation and the object being represented is that of resemblance. We have seen how this is not the case for Nelson Goodman. However, in *Languages of Art*, he does not shed much light onto the specific case of photography. Other philosophers, such as Kendall Walton, have tackled photography more explicitly.

While painting, drawing, and photography are all techniques for producing pictures, for some, photography cannot be thought of in the same way. Some philosophers, for example Kendall Walton, believe, photography is tied to "the enterprise of seeing" and that the advent of photography has given us a "new way of seeing". Walton's thesis is a bold one: for him, the viewer of a photograph literally sees the scene that has been photographed, stressing that we are to take him literally on this:

> *I must warn against watering down this suggestion [...] I am not saying that photography supplements vision [...] Nor is my point that what we see—photographs—are duplicates or doubles or reproductions of objects. My claim is that we see, quite literally, our dead relatives themselves when we look at photographs of them.*[30]

This is Walton's notion of transparency, which claims identical ontology of the photograph and object of representation in photography. This is a difficult yet compelling claim. In the context of painting, no one believes in the identical ontology of the painting and the thing the painting aims to represent, but in photography, Walton is not alone in such claims.

This is why architectural renderings aim to look so realistic. It is not mere resemblance that these representations are after; they do not want to look the way the building might actually be in reality, rather they aim to look like a photograph of the building. This is often achieved by introducing visual effects that occur as a result of the physical interaction of light with the camera's lens, such as the effect of lens flare. For professional photographers, this effect may be undesirable because it results from light being scattered, or flared, in a lens system and points to material imperfections in the lens. Sometimes the effects added to the rendering actually make it look more fantastical and dreamlike, hence less real, but if they emulate physical effects that happen in photography, they are desirable. It is not only because of the common assumption that photography is a faithful reproduction of reality,

but mostly because in looking like a photograph, rather than a realistic rendering, it is as if it were transparent, like a photograph in Walton's account. If a rendering is sufficiently similar to a photograph, it will be as if we are looking at the real building. This is because we all know that images can be faked, but if something was photographed at some point that something existed.[31]

Therefore, in a sense, a rendering will look more realistic not by virtue of how much it resembles the real thing to be constructed, but rather by how closely it provides the illusion of being a photograph of the real thing. In other words, photography elevates the status of an architectural representation that aims to emulate it, because appearing to be a photograph gives the rendering more validity, not by virtue of how realistic it looks but by of how much like a photograph it looks.

An interesting case, which exemplifies this idea even further, is the series of images produced by visual artist Xavier Delory called "photography pilgrimage on modernity". In this series, the artist manipulated photographs of famous buildings, or rather, famous photographs of known buildings, and transformed them in such a way as to make them look vandalized, completely run down, and dilapidated.

This caused a curious commotion in the architecture community; many critics were outraged by the images. Even though it was known they were photoshopped images from existing photographs, they looked so much like the photograph of the building which resided in the collective memory that it was hard to disassociate the photograph from reality. The images were realistic in the sense that they resembled the original iconic photograph. It is almost as if those atrocities had happened to the building just by virtue of it being shown in a photographic-like image.

Photographs will always depict something that exists or has existed, independently of how realistic or non-realistic it may be considered. While architecture and music come into the world, or get produced by their drawings or scores, a painting or a photograph enter into reality by having reality produce them. A score or a drawing are of something that may or may not come into reality. A photograph is always of something that at some point was in the world.[32] It is this relationship between photography and the world, which, at times, is of interest in architectural renderings, hence the wish to emulate the look of a photograph. This emulation was, of course, only possible after the invention of photography, and after the invention of computer-aided design software that made emulating a photograph possible.

III.II Drawing and building in the digital age

Many critics and architects claim that the discipline is in crisis now that drawings are produced mostly aided by the computer. Increasingly, architecture gets thought through and produced directly by drawing in three dimensions, making the production of two-dimensional plans from the three-dimensional model very immediate. So, the two-dimensional drawings that were so painstakingly slow to produce accurately by hand emerge as a result of a cut in a three-dimensionally built digital model. There is still work to be done to these cuts for them to read as plans, but in the eyes of many—architects and non-architects—this ability to produce drawings from a digital model is detrimental to the discipline and is putting architectural representation in crisis. In academia, there are increasing complaints regarding students not knowing how to draw plans and sections anymore, given the ubiquity and reliance on the computer. Another concern is generated by the ability to infinitely zoom into a digital model, in a way that was not possible in hand-drawing with the limitations set by the paper's surface and the thickness of the pencil's lead. Digital drawings' zoomable capacity has resulted in a loss of control of the sense of scale, distance, and size. In addition, modeling in perspective and a relatively quick ability to output perspectival renderings provide deceptive views of the object being represented.

The use of the computer has certainly made the production of drawings faster and in some respects easier, and there has undoubtedly been some loss of traditional modes of drawing. It has paralleled what happened to painting with the invention of photography; it is just easier and much faster to capture details of texture, light, and shadow in a photograph than in painting. Therefore, rather than seeing it as a detrimental intrusion to the artform, the introduction of new forms of production (and reproduction) can be seen as opening new possibilities for the artform. Photography liberated painters from having to work so attentively on realism, or slave for hours over the detail of how a drop of water reflected the sun at a particular moment in time. It spearheaded the work of abstraction and experimentation that pushed the possibilities of painting as an artform in new directions, and produced new abstract ways of representing ideas. In the same way that photography liberated painting and allowed it to discover new directions, computer-aided drawing should be viewed as liberating to the architect, who is no longer bound to the drawing table with ink and vellum to produce precise drawings and representations. Although the production of these drawings is by no means obsolete, the computer has just permitted more exploration of the discipline's representational capacities, much like photography has not made realism in painting obsolete.

With each new technique that is discovered, new representational possibilities are uncovered too. This is also the case with the use of the computer. When digitally produced drawings are critiqued for using the computer as a means for architectural representation at the expense of the art of drawing by hand, these critiques are often rooted in understanding the computer as a technique of representation and not of production of architectural thinking, both for the creator and the observer of the drawings. To claim that computer software allows us to think differently might seem an abomination to some, but if it enables new representational techniques, then new ways of seeing and thinking are enabled as well.

Endnotes

1 Architecture is a discipline with a significant technical component but here, and in Goodman's work, it is nonetheless understood as an artistic practice.

2 While Goodman coined this distinction as applied to artistic practices, he works off of the existing English terms of *allograph* and *autograph;* the former refers to a document written by someone other than those who signed it, the latter is the unique signature of one person.

3 To quote Goodman directly: "There are, indeed, compositions falsely purporting to be by Haydn as there are paintings falsely purporting to be by Rembrandt; but of the London Symphony, unlike the Lucretia, there can be no forgeries." *Languages of Art*, p 112.

4 Goodman produces a theory of notation that differentiates types of artistic practices. *Languages of Art*, p 112.

5 The case of dance for instance is interesting because there is no canonical form of notation, even though the finding of one has certainly been attempted (the best known being Labanotation invented by Rudolf Laban). But as it is an "ephemeral art" it fits into Goodman's definition of allographic art.

6 However, Goodman does not use the term "pictorial", instead he refers to it as "sketch".

7 Goodman, *Languages of Art*, p 219.

8 Although he claims that differentiation and density are not opposites of each other, analog and digital are opposites. Goodman, *Languages of Art*, p 161.

9 "a system is analog if syntactically and semantically dense". Ibid, p 160.

10 Goodman's theory of notation is more elaborate than this statement; he identifies five different aspects that make a notation a notation, but for the purposes of discussing the mixed case of architectural representation and keeping the argument more focused we are not engaging in the elaboration of Goodman's theory.

11 "Diagrams are flat and static models". Goodman, *Languages of Art*, p 173.

12 In its broader sense, including models and other modes of representation.

13 Robin Evans, "Architectural Projection" found in *Translations from Drawing to Building*, Cambridge, MA: MIT Press, 1997, p 21. There are exceptions, of course, such as with particular types of architectural intervention, such as design-build where the design and the building happen simultaneously.

14 This is most obviously seen in the case of music where works from different time periods can be performed. In architecture, a recent example is the redevelopment of the southern tip of Roosevelt Island in New York.

15 Importantly, Goodman defines what he means by notation through the five technical rules.

16 Goodman, "How Buildings Mean" in *Critical Inquiry*, vol 11, no 4 (June 1985), p 642.

17 This comparison can also be seen as illustrated in the diagram.

18 These tools are not restricted to drawing, but encompass also text, not just in the form of specifications for the built (what Goodman refers to as "script"), but theoretical texts, and treatises.

19 Stan Allen, *Mapping the Unmappable*, London: Routledge, 2003, p 31.

20 Ibid, p 33.

21 Goodman, *Languages of Art*, p 128.

22 These plans do not recognize how Roosevelt Island has evolved in the past 30 years, or the asymmetries present on either shore. The symmetrical imposition culminates at the tip of the island with a concrete cube that inhibits the panoramic views available before, in an introverted gesture to commemorate the white male who already holds the island's name.

23 Goodman is considering the differentiation between artistic practices. This kind of construct would not be classified as architecture understood as an artistic practice. It is something else, mere construction, possibly.

24 "that architecture may be allographic in its plan stage but autographic in its second, built stage." Kirk Pillow, "Did Goodman's Distinction Survive LeWitt?" in *The Journal of Aesthetics and Art Criticism*, 61:4 (Fall 2003).

25 Allen, *Mapping the Unmappable*, p 40.

26 This is also what Stan Allen claims.

27 "The renderings made to convey the appearance of the finished building are sketches." Goodman uses the term sketch to denote an architectural rendering, so I am keeping this assimilation here but they are different things: "a sketch is a drawing done in preparation for the final representation, while a rendering aims to render the scene in the same way as it would be rendered in real life, and it has a sense of finality to it that a sketch does not. [...] Realistic representation, in brief, depends not upon imitation or illusion or information but upon inculcation." Goodman, *Languages of Art*, p 218.

28 For Goodman, since the mechanical reproducibility of a representation did not really have anything to do with its authenticity, as it did for Walter Benjamin, for now I am leaving aside whether the rendering was produced by hand or with the aid of computer software. Even though I do not think it is an unimportant distinction.

29 Which may actually make some realistic, unappealing elements not be shown.

30 Kendall Walton, "Depiction, Perception, and Imagination: Responses to Richard Wollheim" in *Marvelous Images: On Values and the Arts*. Oxford University Press, pp 251–252.

31 Photographs can of course also be faked, and Walton is very aware of this too. But, in it being a photograph, there will always be aspects of it that once existed.

32 This does not mean that a photograph cannot be imbued with ideology and things that are ephemeral (beliefs), but it is a major difference between an architectural drawing and a photograph.

Bibliography

Allen, Stan. *Practice, Architecture, Technique and Representation*. London: Routledge, 2003.

Bazin, André. "The Ontology of the Photographic Image" in *What Is Cinema?* Translated by Hugh Gray, vol 1. Berkeley and Los Angeles: University of California Press, 1967, pp 9–22.

Benjamin, Walter. "The Work of Art in the Age of Mechanical Reproduction" in *Illuminations*. New York: Schocken, 1968.

D'cruz, Jason and P.D. Magnus. "Are Digital Images Allographic?" in *The Journal of Aesthetics and Art Criticism*, 72:4 (Fall 2014), pp 417–427.

Evans, Robin. *Translation from Drawing to Building*. Cambridge, MA: MIT Press, 1997.

Goodman, Nelson. "How Buildings Mean" in *Critical Inquiry*, vol 11, no 4 (June 1985), pp 642–653.

Goodman, Nelson. *Languages of Art: An Approach to a Theory of Symbols*, Indianapolis: Hackett Publishing Company, 1976.

Goodman, Nelson. *Of Mind and Other Matters*. Cambridge, MA: Harvard University Press, 1984.

Gombrich, Ernst. *Art and Illusion*. London: Phaidon Press, 1960.

Pillow, Kirk. "Did Goodman's Distinction Survive LeWitt?" in *The Journal of Aesthetics and Art Criticism*, 61:4 (Fall 2003), pp 365–380.

Walton, Kendall. "Depiction, Perception, and Imagination: Responses to Richard Wollheim" in *Marvelous Images: On Values and the Arts*. Oxford University Press, 2008, pp 143–156.

Illustrations

Analog and digital, p 122. Sketches by author.

Different notational systems, p 123. Internet images and plan by author.

Diagram on allographic-architecture-autographic works, p 124. Sketches by Ian Gordon.

Le Corbusier's Carpenter Center floor plan, p 126. Found on archdaily.com, March 13, 2011.

Architectural projections systems, p 128. Francis Ching, *Design and Drawing.*

Renderings of Dubrovnik housing project, p 130. By e+i studio, showing added lens flare effect.

Le Corbusier's Villa Savoye and image by Xavier Delory, p 131. Found on designboom.com.

mag.net performance installation

2012

MAG.NET was a collaborative architecture-dance project between e+i studio and Human Kinetics Movement Arts, with whom we had collaborated on previous performance installations. The theme of magnetism was initiated by Yana Schnitzler, the group's artistic director, and together we delved into a year-long research project to study and explore ways to materialize this invisible force. In our research we soon realized that even very potent magnets had subtle movements, and magnetism in large-scale or body environments could easily be missed. So, it was key for the architectural piece to increase the effect of magnetic forces between bodies—it had to augment the performance.

The design explored the interaction between the body and the environment by making visible the effects of magnetism through choreographed dance movements. It also aimed at engaging the casual passerby by activating the street during performances, with audiences gathering within the space and spilling out into the street.

The main feature was a web-like interactive form made from off-the-shelf biodegradable black rubber bands and metal paper clips, suspended and stretched into a reactive form within the Tribeca gallery space. The flexible web became a self-regulating form that negotiated the unique configuration of the gallery, the tensile nature of the network of rubber bands, and the influence of gravity on the entire web.

The mesh was reconfigured by the movements of the dancers, who had magnets embedded within tight-fitting costumes. It took over one hour to fit the dancers each night because the magnets were incredibly strong, and we had to keep them from magnetizing with each other. The interaction of the performers and the suspended web activated the magnets, pulling the web to their bodies.

The web became a domain of interaction, each dancer being a point of magnetic attraction. As the dancers moved, so did the web, pushing and pulling the network, with ripple-like effects. It became an interactive realm of movement and changing perception as the dancers transformed and shaped the space with their movements.

What was interesting for us was that we could only roughly anticipate the form of the web and its behavior, much like observing nonhuman animal behaviors—they are very difficult to fully predict. The form that we designed was a kind of notation, but the ultimate form was contingent on the actualities of the joint performance of the space, materiality, gravity, and bodies in the space, including the audience.

Project data

- **Location** White Space Gallery, New York City
- **Design and fabrication** Eva Perez de Vega + Ian Gordon
- **Research Assistants** Aviva Novick, Flavia Bertorello and Patricia Niclos
- **Fabrication Assistance** Siena Gordon, Harry Schnitzler and Yana Schnitzler
- **Human kinetics movement arts** Yana Schnitzler, artistic director; Masumi Kishimoto, Akiko Bo Nishijima, dancers
- **Performance photos** Harry Schnitzler
- **Organization** Manhattan Community Arts Fund, supported by the New York City Department of Cultural Affairs in partnership with the City Council

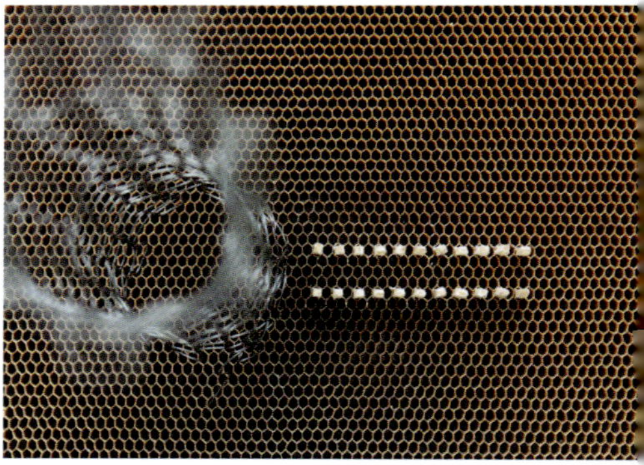

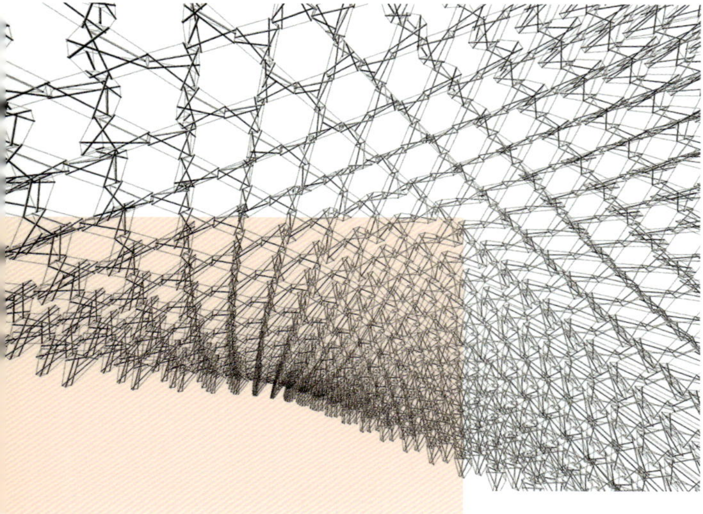

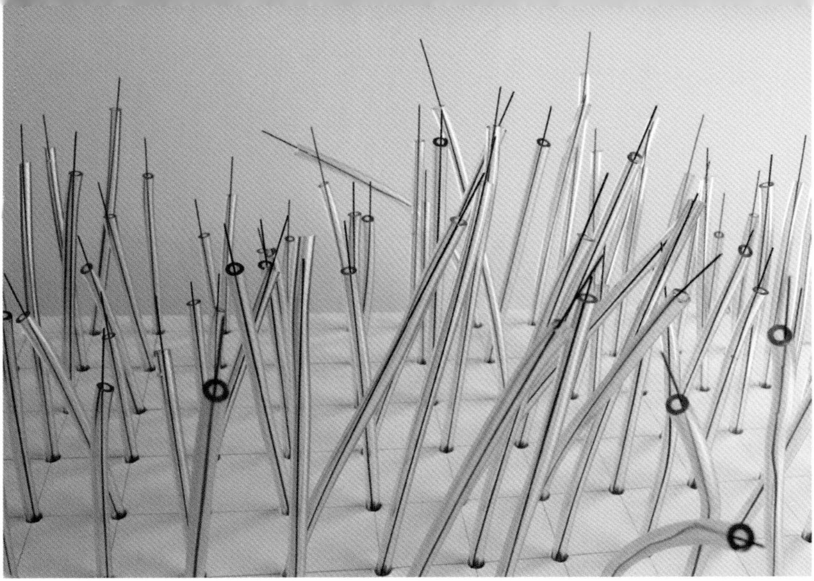

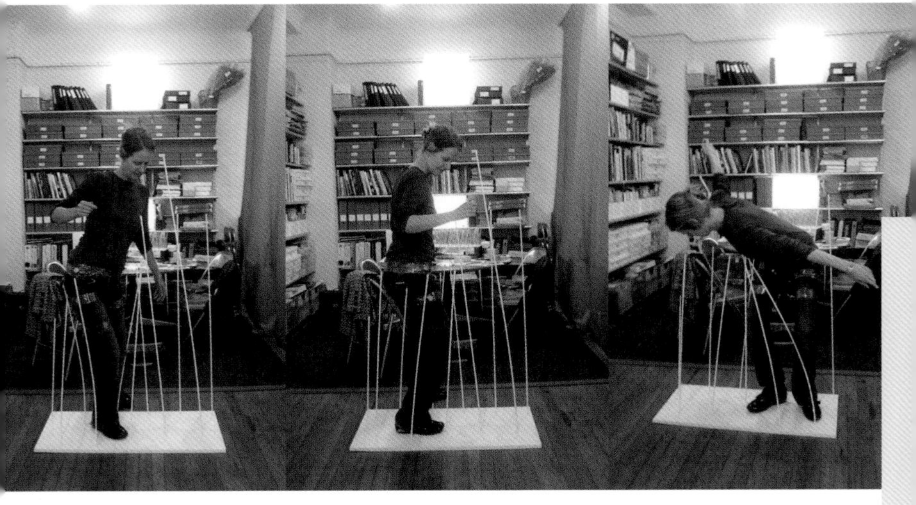

nuages performance installation

2010

In close collaboration with NuDance Theater, this project was conceived of as a layered soft space that was an intimate evocation of mist and condensation. This cloud-like installation, located in a gallery on a busy Midtown Manhattan street, was materialized through hanging nylon strings of varying densities and lengths that resulted in changing degrees of transparency. The goal was to create a flowing liquid space that would engage the city and the performers by having the physical elements of the space affect their movements and in turn their movements affected by the possibilities of the space.

We were interested in transforming the generic rectangular space into a soft-space with nuance and difference where an ephemeral ambiance was tied to the narrative of the dance performances producing a series of perceptual effects. The work interfaces the very open and visible quality of the gallery with a wish to create secluded and hidden zones, in which dancers moving in and around the installation could appear and disappear, engendering an ambiguous "in-between" zone where exterior (audience) and interior (dancers) would meet. The limits of the rectangular gallery space were visually dissolved through the layered strings, giving both audience and performers a sensation of an endlessly enveloping and boundary-less inner world.

After an intense period of material experimentation aimed at achieving the effect of "materializing mist" we rented a studio space with NuDance in the Brooklyn Fire Proof building, where the dancers choreographed the performance while we built the components of the installation. It was a beautiful symbiosis between the dance and the built space created to support movement and a choreographed narrative. The installation was moved panel by panel to the LAB gallery one freezing New York evening, after preparing the space to receive the sixteen massive panels with the preassembled string choreography. Given the corner storefront exposure, our installation also had an urban quality that was lit at night, glowing into the streetscape, and engaging passersby to stop and look.

The project combined the allographic nature of dance performance and the ambiguous qualities of an architectural installation. The installation was modeled and designed digitally, translated into built form and ultimately given to the built world as the materialization of an idea.

Project data

- **Location** Midtown Manhattan, New York City
- **Design and fabrication** Eva Perez de Vega + Ian Gordon
- **Assistant** Flavia Bertorello
- **nu dance theater** Sophie Bortolussi and Eva Perrotta
- **Photography** Brandon Jacobs-Mills
- **Installation assistants** Flavia Bertorello, Lauren Greenland, Adrienne Reynolds, Jacinda Ross and Monica Wynn
- **Organization** Lower Manhattan Cultural Council, MCAF, supported by the New York City Department of Cultural Affairs in partnership with the City Council

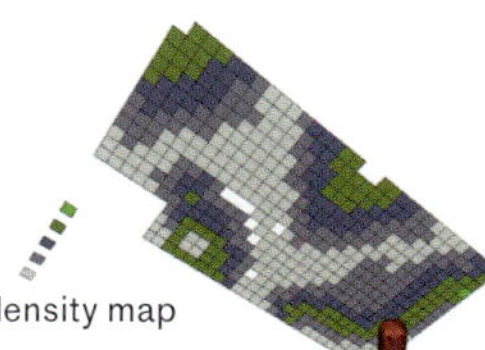

density map

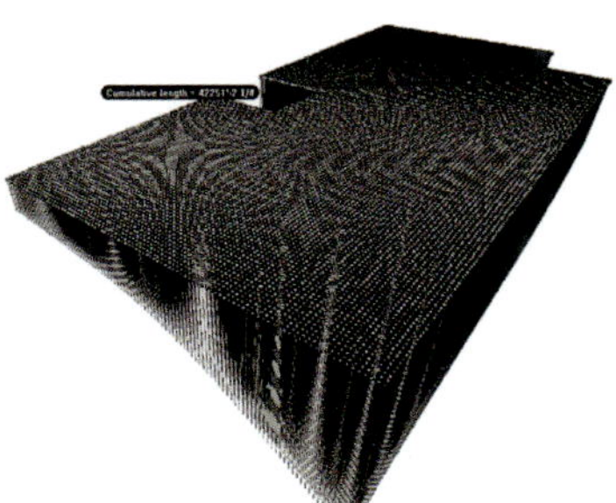

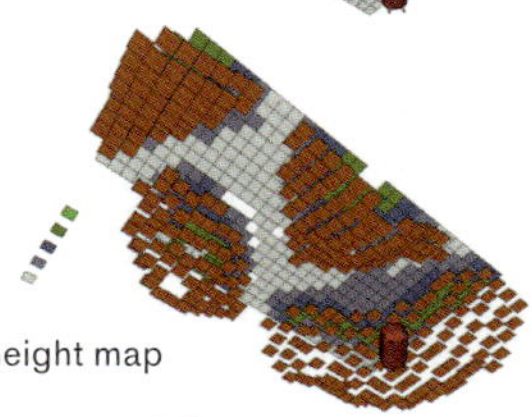

height map

cord lengths

fluid adagio public plaza

2010

The project created an artificial landscape whose surfaces invited novel ways of inhabiting and moving through it. In turn, the landscape acted as a daily register of movement, with traces left on the sand producing everchanging striated designs.

The project was a performative piece in itself but also brought performance into the urban center by providing a public space in an abandoned lot for events to revitalize the area. At timed moments throughout the day, there was a changing choreography of sand striations left on the dry garden—a combination of automated and handcrafted raked patterns inscribed on the sand. We called these "striating choreography events", which were dialogues between the sand and the mechanical means of reproducing patterns on it.

Utah is known to the world for its intricately carved canyon landscapes, which are multicolored strata-scapes from millions of years of wind, water, and geologic movements. Perhaps lesser known is Utah's institutions' commitment to research technological advancement. Our proposal for this public plaza brought together this dual consideration; while heavily inspired by the evocative striated landscapes of the canyons that mark human activity at a geological scale, it also relied on technology as a means of efficiently and sustainably constructing the proposal.

Inspired by Utah's striated desert landscape, in the way that the canyon is carved by the river to reveal its strata, we proposed an organization based on the notion of striation. Our strategy for Fluid Adagio Public Space is to generate mound-like elements that are carved to incorporate different seating and lounging positions. The project combines a series of fixed yet articulated seating typologies within an evolving and transforming urban landscape, or dune-scape. After the sand is displaced by movement during the day, there are intermittent performative moments of "re-writing" the traces, using a mechanical rake at the perimeter that can re-comb the striations into emerging patterns on the sand-scape.

The local sand that covers most of the plaza acts as a mechanism to "trace" the movement of the day—much like a notation that anticipates a melody—these traces are at once a reference to the community engaging with it and an anticipation of the possibilities that public spaces afford.

Project data

- **Location** Salt Lake City, Utah
- **Design** Eva Perez de Vega + Ian Gordon
- **Assistant** Flavia Bertorello
- **Organization** AIA Utah, Fluid Adagio Installation

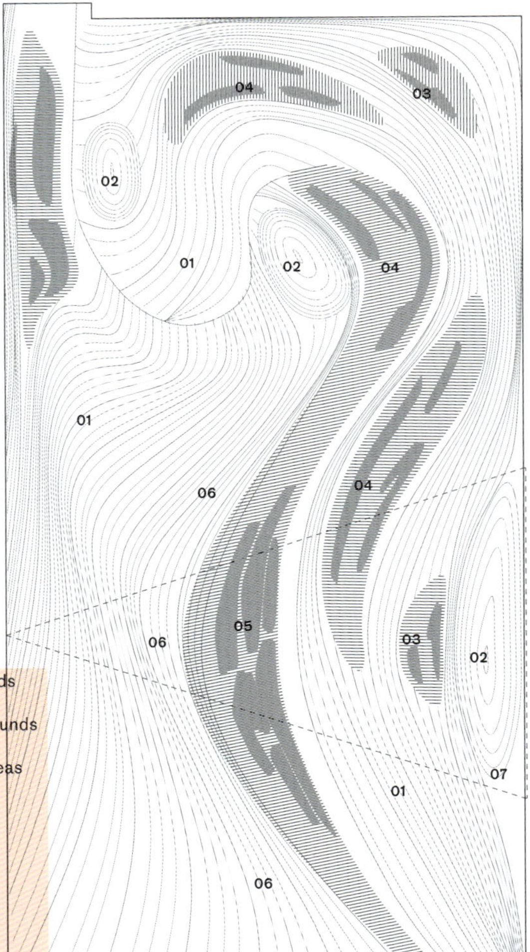

plan of striated landscape

01 raked sand landscape
02 slight dips in sandscape
03 small seating/lounging mounds formed with wood profiles
04 medium seating/lounging mounds formed with wood profiles
05 canopy element for vendor areas formed with wood profiles
06 vendor areas
07 projection screen

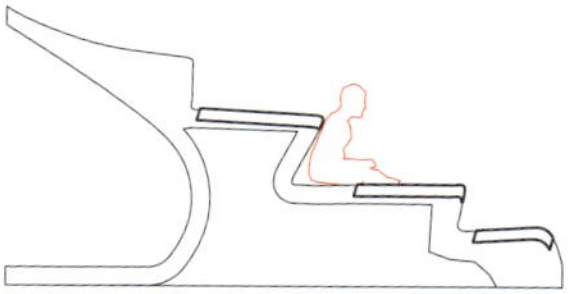

wave form

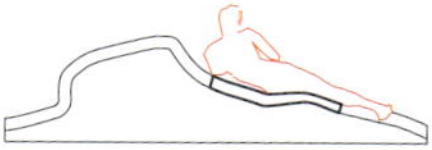

mound form

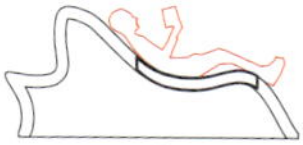

valley form

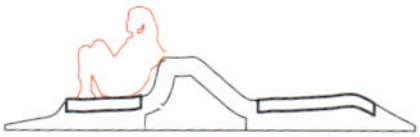

ripple form

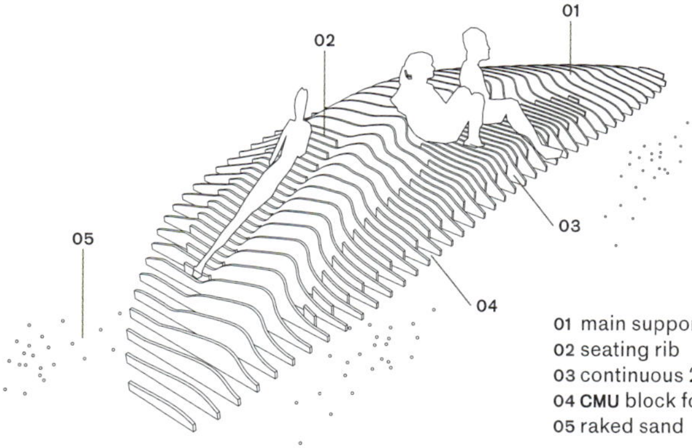

01 main support rib
02 seating rib
03 continuous 2X bracing
04 CMU block foundation
05 raked sand

south street seaport museum

2008

This project was a speculative re-examination of the South Street Seaport site, a strip of land and water along the East River waterfront starting at the base of the Brooklyn Bridge.

The project posited a way to seamlessly connect the city to the river by blurring the distinction between land and water with a submerged space for the museum just beneath the level of the river. Acknowledging the fraught action of occupying nonhuman territory below the water's surface, the project aims to also foster new ecosystems that can flourish by using the submerged walls of the underwater structure. Oysters would be part of these ecosystems, acting as a natural filtration system to clean the surrounding water of chemicals and pollutants in the East River.

New programmatic and experiential opportunities would be enabled by slipping the ground plane below water level and extending it beyond the shoreline. The project literally utilizes the East River as the project's facade, as a fluid plateau filtering light to the spaces below.

Skylight oculus openings in the structure provide completely new perceptions of Brooklyn Bridge from below water level, framing unusual views of the bridge. In turn, looking downward from Brooklyn Bridge provided an overview of the building roofscape, submerged within the East River.

This project was a prototype for future waterfront projects, a representation of possible realities waiting for the dynamic and unpredictable natural elements such as wind, water, and sun to activate it in the world.

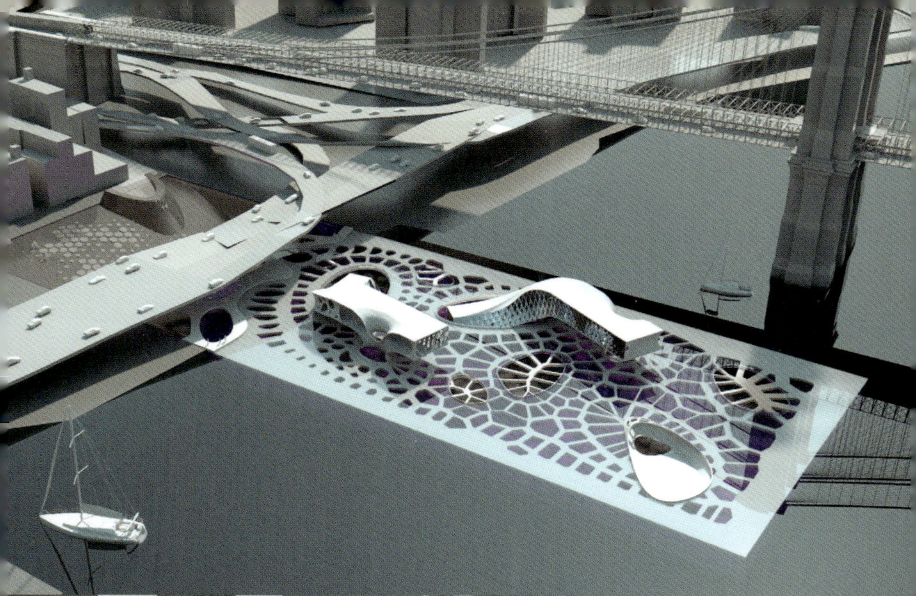
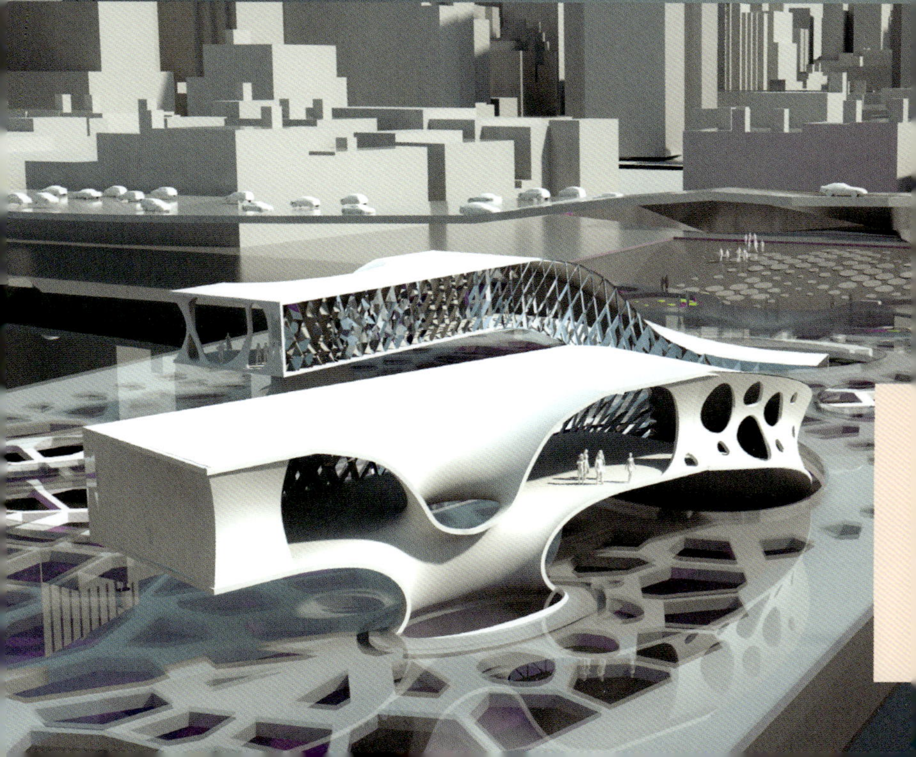

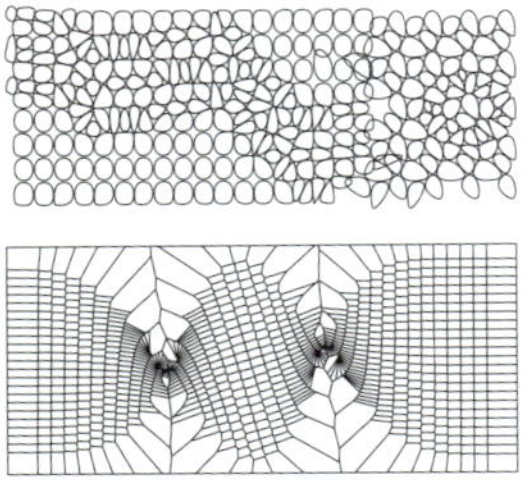

voronoi partition tests

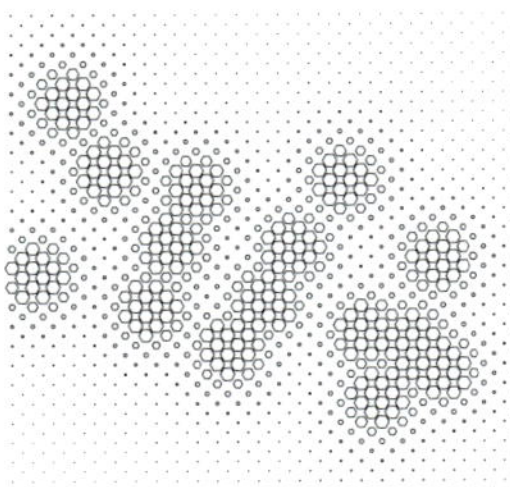

gradient scaling test

voronoi partitioning +
gradient scaling

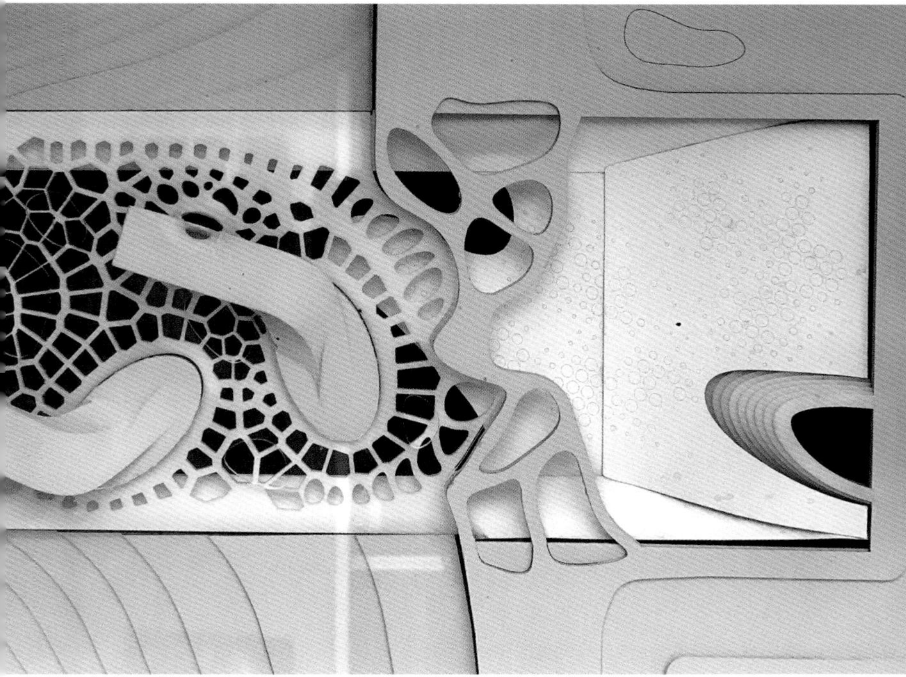

Project data

- **Location** New York City
- **Design** Ian Gordon
- **Posthuman render** Ziyu Chen
- **Organization** Emerging New York Architects Committee (ENYA), AIA NY Chapter

OPPOSITE In a speculative future scenario without human presence on this site, the project would be the anchor and the start of biodiverse life on land and water. With warming climates and ice caps melting, the East River would most likely be like seawater, known today as "freshwater salinization syndrome". This would allow sealions and manta rays to join these transformed territories.

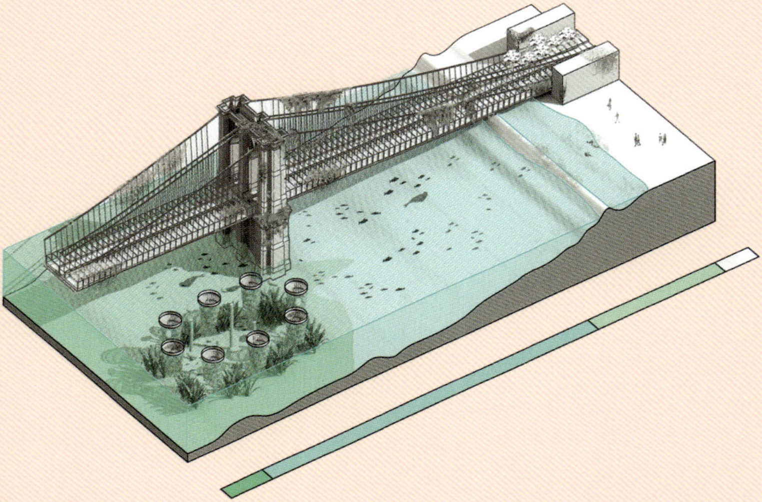

2050 alternative

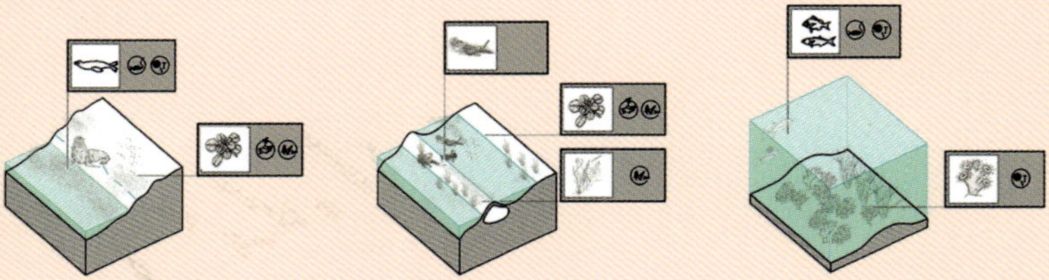

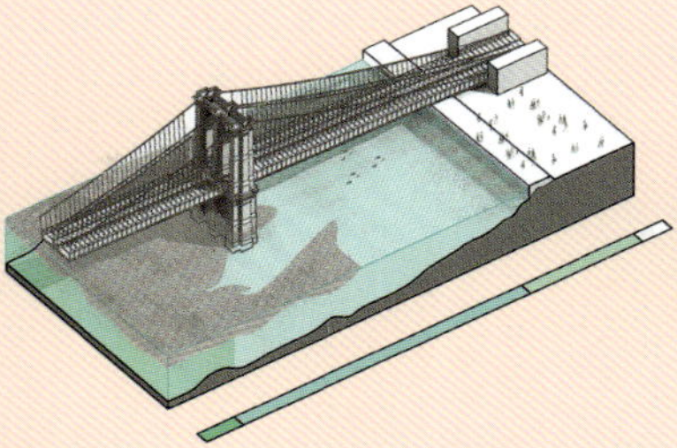

2050

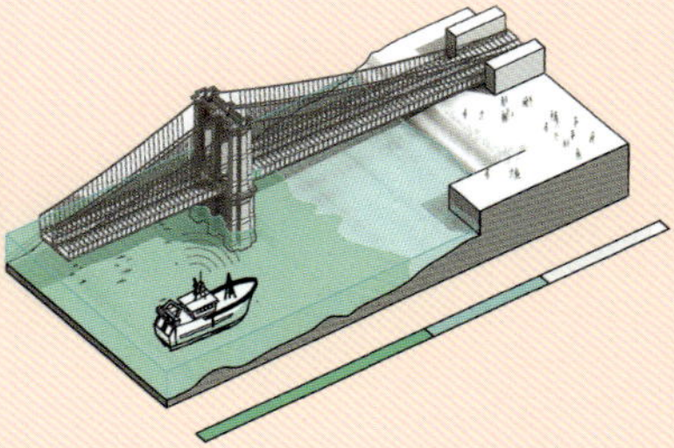

present

Eva Perez de Vega is an architect, designer, and educator. She holds a Masters and a Bachelors degree in Architecture from the University of Madrid, School of Architecture (ETSAM) specializing in Building Structures, and a Masters in Philosophy from The New School for Social Research, where she is currently in the PhD program in Philosophy. Prior to establishing e+i studio, Eva was lead design architect at Reiser + Umemoto, RUR Architecture PC.

Eva has been teaching architecture and design while practicing professionally and is currently professor at Pratt Institute School of Architecture where she teaches thesis, and at Parsons School of Design where she has been teaching architecture and design since 2004. She has previously taught at the University of Pennsylvania Landscape Architecture School and Princeton School of Architecture. Originally from Rome, Italy, with a British-Spanish background, she has lived in New York City since 2001.

Ian Gordon is a licensed architect in New York State with professional experience working in New York, North Carolina, and Madrid, Spain. He received his Master's Degree in Advanced Architectural Design (AAD) and graduated with honors from Columbia University. He holds a Bachelor's degree in Architecture from NC State University and has a background in Fine Arts. Prior to e+i studio, Ian worked as an architect for Studio Daniel Libeskind working on a range of international projects.

Ian is an adjunct professor at New York School of Interior Design (NYSID), Parsons School of Design, and New York City College of Technology (NYCCT). He teaches a wide range of Architecture, Interior Design, and 3D modeling courses. Ian grew up living in various countries in Africa, as well as Rome, Italy. Originally from Manila, Philippines, with an American-French background, Ian traveled significantly before settling in New York City in 2001.

is an architecture and design practice based in New York City, founded by partners Eva Perez de Vega + Ian Gordon.

The work of e+i studio engages the built environment's capacity to contribute affirmatively to the well-being of our human species while also taking non-human life into account. A multi-species approach to architecture is accompanied by an interest in crafting spaces, environments, and objects that promote interaction and choreograph movement through carefully sequenced spatial relations. Informed by a background both principals share in movement-related practices, the work of e+i emerges from the exploration of the performance of matter and bodies in space. Architecture is thus understood as a material manifestation of choreographed space within the natural environment that sustains it.

Eva, a native of Rome with British-Spanish nationality, and Ian, a native of the Philippines with an American-French background, met while in high school in Rome. Spending every possible moment sketching in piazzas and churches, both partners felt these early years had a deep impact on them, which helped forge a shared passion for design and architecture that Eva + Ian bring to every project the joint practice undertakes.

At e+i we believe that collaboration and interdisciplinary exchange are a vital component of the design process. We work closely with clients as collaborators, incorporating expertise from various disciplines in order to find unique and environmental solutions for any design problem. Each project demands a unique approach and is considered from a multi-faceted perspective, balancing social and environmental parameters, aesthetics, innovation, and the realities of budget and fabrication.

We are particularly interested in projects that engage the public, that are meaningful for the communities they serve, and that bring people together, providing awareness of the importance the constructed environment holds on our well-being as a human species, living within natural environments that support and sustain us.

We approach architecture as an interdisciplinary practice that emerges from the exploration of the performance of matter and bodies in space. For us, architecture is a material manifestation of choreographed space. In other words, we seek to propose solutions that engage all users, is performative, and takes into account change in time and use.

Artifice Press Limited
The Maple Building
39–51 Highgate Road
London NW5 1RT
United Kingdom
—
+44 (0)20 8371 4047
office@artificeonline.com
www.artificeonline.com

Designed by Rachel Pfleger
Edited by Kim Scott
Printed in the United Kingdom by DG3 Leycol.

ISBN 978-1-911339-44-1

British Library in Cataloguing Data. A CIP record for this book is available from the British Library.

Artifice